How to Get Out of Debt

by

Ted Nicholas

First Printing—January, 1976
Second Printing—July, 1977
Third Printing (revised)—May, 1980
Fourth Printing—December, 1980

Library of Congress Catalog Card No. 75-45878
ISBN: 0-913864-60-9

Published by Enterprise Publishing, Inc.
725 Market Street
Wilmington, Delaware 19801

Printed in the United States of America

Table of Contents

Debt Readjustment Plan
(Chapter 13) For Individuals With Regular Income

Bankruptcy

Filling Out The Forms

Acknowledgements

Individuals who have made valuable contributions to this book include the entire staff of Enterprise Publishing, Inc.; Joseph Hutton, for suggestions on the manuscript and invaluable research; Robert H. Blumberg, for helpful suggestions on the subject of bankruptcy; Sylvan N. Levy, Jr., for encouragement and moral support. A good job on the charts was done by Margaret R. Buchanan. Special thanks to Beverly Horning Natrin on this fully-revised edition.

A special acknowledgement to the many hundreds of people in the United States who, within the last two hundred years, have worked toward a more humane approach toward debtors. Included in this list are the framers of the U. S. Constitution, which gave Congress the power to establish laws on bankruptcy, and countless lawyers, judges, and lay people who have made contributions toward the elimination of debtors' prisons, as well as laws for the orderly handling and disposition of matters arising between debtors and creditors. Their efforts have enabled many honest men and women to overcome debt problems and gain a fresh start, a fundamental necessity in a dynamic free enterprise economic system.

Ted Nicholas

Introduction

In recent years, the subject of managing both business and personal debt, and the related issue of bankruptcy has been receiving increased attention by individuals who might not previously have given the subject a passing thought. Knowledge of this subject is valuable to every thoughtful individual who, in order to survive, must cope with a world in financial turmoil. One is forced to adjust to severe economic and financial pressures comparable to the Great Depression of the 1930's with possibly worse things on the horizon.

It is not our intention to advocate declaring bankruptcy at the first sign of individual financial problems. A knowledge of bankruptcy matters and related laws may enable you to avoid it altogether. On the other hand, we do not consider bankruptcy to be necessarily a sign of immorality, irresponsibility, or ignorance.

A review of bankruptcy reveals many famous individuals who have been outstanding in their respective fields: Mickey Rooney, Dick Haymes, Lance Alworth, George Sanders, Craig Morton, Pat Boone—all have experienced bankruptcy. The above individuals achieved success in careers other than business. But how do we explain that some of the most successful business people of all time, such as Henry Ford, Bernard Gimbel, Milton Hershey, and Frank Woolworth had at least one experience with bankruptcy? To build the giant business enterprises that these individuals did, required great courage and willingness to take risks. Individuals with these entrepreneurial characteristics *do* have a greater chance of going bankrupt at some time in their careers.

Great financial genius does not seem to offer any guarantee against bankruptcy, either. One of the few investment people who foresaw the 1929 stock market crash was Bernard Baruch, a financial advisor to a number of Presidents and a man who experienced bankruptcy not once, but a number of times.

Wealthy family background is not any guarantee against bankruptcy. In one of the most spectacular bankruptcy cases in recent years, a wealthy family name proved to be a key factor in *causing* financial disaster. In 1970, Lammot duPont Copeland, the son of the then-Chairman of the Board of the huge DuPont Company, entered bankruptcy court in a case which was to result in claims of over $50 million. A major part of Mr. Copeland's problem was that his duPont name made it so easy for him to borrow. In most cases, the debts were incurred by companies in which Mr. Copeland had an interest and had signed his name to guarantee repayment.

Perhaps you would like some insight into the picture ahead of us.

The first part of this book deals with some of the economic background that we consider relevant in putting the problem of bankruptcy in perspective. Part of the material is historical, but much of it deals with broad economic forces that have recently aggravated financial problems of individuals and businesses. It is our view that the individual must know the size of the economic problems facing the country today to avoid being caught in the accompanying financial difficulties.

After dealing with the external factors that are principal causes in economic and financial problems, then we go on to discuss the problems which individuals seem to create for themselves. Great emphasis is placed on wise consumer purchasing and personal financial management.

An entire section is devoted to involuntary bankruptcy and the desirability of avoiding it. The pitfalls which can trigger involuntary bankruptcy are explored in detail.

A full chapter reviews the subject of how individuals with regular incomes can benefit from debt readjustment plans. This is a method of working out financial problems without going through bankruptcy. The procedure is described, and sample forms with explanations are included. Also included are the most commonly asked questions and answers about this procedure.

The next major issue addressed is voluntary bankruptcy, including important advantages to both debtors and creditors. Described are the basic steps to be followed and the most commonly asked questions.

A full section is comprised of detailed descriptions of forms to be used, definitions, and procedures to be followed.

Business considerations are contained in a separate chapter. Proprietorships, partnerships, and corporations are covered.

Our goal is to maintain a neutral position on the subject of bankruptcy. It is our view that this book will give you the necessary background to enable you to make your own individual decisions, based on your particular circumstances.

Historical Background

The history of bankruptcy is as old as civilization itself. Reference to creditor/debtor relationships can be found in the Old Testament, and scholars of ancient history have found the subject mentioned even earlier than the time of Moses in the Old Testament.

Much of the history of bankruptcy has been a sad commentary on humanity. In Mesopotamia, one of the earliest civilizations, a bankrupt person might find himself enslaved for debt or, more commonly, might sell his wife or children into slavery in order to pay off his debts. In Ancient Greece, debt was classified as a crime comparable to murder. Even in later periods, debtors might be required to sell their children as slaves. Hindu law permitted a creditor to kill or maim a debtor. In Ancient Rome, bankruptcy was punishable by enslavement or death. When the creditors disagreed on the alternative, the bankrupt person could be dismembered with each creditor claiming his portion.

Punishment by death for debt continued into the Middle Ages. In parts of Spain, as late as 1360, the money changer who was unable to pay his creditors was beheaded in front of his bank. In France, punishment was particularly severe for fraudulent bankruptcy. The Code of Commerce in 1673 provided the death penalty for the fraudulent bankrupt person. The penalty was, apparently, not carried out swiftly. A record of one such bankrupt individual tells of his being led through the street, clad only in a shirt, with a rope around his neck. He was attached to the public pillory for three days, fined heavily, and then sent to the galleys for nine years.

A history of bankruptcy would also reveal that governments, while making laws punishing debtors, were often at the root of the problem. One of the largest bankruptcies of Medieval Times was the collapse of the Fugger Financial Empire in 1607, after two centuries of growth. Contributing to the fall of the firm were defaults on debts by Spain and France in 1557, followed by similar defaults by the Dutch and Belgian governments in subsequent decades. Although the Fuggers did not have many outside partners, their failure ruined so many clients that a larger debtors' prison had to be built in Augsburg to hold all of them.

Still, the history of bankruptcy has not been a completely negative story. Even when a person could be enslaved for debt, it was not necessarily a life sentence. One of the oldest legal codes, that of Hammurabi, provided "three years shall they work in the house of the buyer and in the fourth year he shall fix their liberty." Enslavement of one Hebrew by another might also be light and temporary, as indicated by the following quote from the Old Testament:

> *"If thy brother be waxen poor and be sold unto thee and shall serve thee six years after which he and his family were free to depart."*

The Hebrew laws also provided certain protection to the debtor by ensuring that he could not be deprived of basic necessities. This offered the precedent for what we now call "exempt assets." When the Hebrew slave was set free, he was not to be "sent away empty," but furnished "liberally out of the flock, and out of the winepress." If a person's cloak was taken from him as security on a loan, it had to be returned to him at nightfall. A creditor could not take a debtor's millstone, because this would deprive the family of its daily food.

Debtor prisons existed during the early history of the United States, but the shortage of labor reduced their importance relative to that in Europe. The colony of Georgia was established in 1732 as a debtors' refuge. The "indentured servant" was common in our early history and represented mostly voluntary debt slaves working off their passage to America. Starting with Kentucky in 1821, debtor prisons were abolished in this country one by one.

The Constitution gave Congress the power to establish laws on the subject of bankruptcy, and three times (in 1800, 1841, and 1867), Congress did enact a law. In each case, however, the law was repealed after the economic crises that had triggered it passed. During most of these years, state laws predominated, but these were not uniform. The present bankruptcy act was passed in 1978, to take effect October 1, 1979, and contains some provisions to be phased in by 1984. This act repealed the Federal Bankruptcy Act of 1898, which had been modified in 1938.

The nature of our present bankruptcy law was summarized by a Supreme Court Justice in 1873:

> *"The very essence of a national bankruptcy system is the doing away with pre-existing contracts, the prevention of preference among creditors, . . . the distribution of assets of a debtor upon the principle that equality among creditors and the making of such reasonable exemptions of property to the bankrupt as will keep him from absolute poverty, give him support and educate his family, and make him a good and useful citizen."*

Although major changes in bankruptcy laws are not frequent, gradual changes do occur. Within the last several years, debtors have been given increased protection by the Consumer Credit Protection Act and the Truth in Lending Act. One objective of this legislation was to restrict the practice of wage garnishment, which often leads to bankruptcy.

Government Controls

This renewed interest in bankruptcy must surprise many government and private economists who believed not too many years ago that economic cycles and their resultant financial crises could be controlled, if not banished, by the government. It was claimed that with the safety of bank deposits insured by the government, there would be no danger of such "runs on the banks" as occurred during the Great Depression. Also, the banks have not one, but at least three, governmental regulatory agencies keeping check on them. One might reasonably be justified in thinking that our banking system is safe beyond question. Yet, it is in serious trouble.

The Social Security System was expected to be a guarantee that our Senior Citizens would not be destitute in their later years. A deduction for Social Security was supposed to be like an insurance premium. Unfortunately, it has proved, instead, to be one of the most rapidly increasing taxes in recent years. There is no end in sight if the system is to avoid bankruptcy itself. Dramatically increasing taxes, including Social Security taxes, have been a major deterrent to individuals attempting to provide their own retirement funds.

Unemployment was also expected to be controllable at low levels. First, government expenditures were supposed to stabilize the economy, so that wide economic swings could not occur. Second, an increasing percentage of our work force was employed in public and quasi-public industries, which was supposed to maintain, or even increase, employment during economic downturns. There would still be a few unemployed, but didn't we have unemployment compensation to take care of the temporarily unemployed? And didn't we have welfare to take care of those unable to work for other reasons?

The Myth of Economic Stabilizers

Unfortunately, these economic stabilizers have not only been overrated, they have been completely misrepresented to the citizenry of the U. S. and severely abused by many. The government has always found it more politically popular to stimulate the economy by new programs, than to provide such programs on a "pay-as-you-go" basis. Consequently, a deficit budget has been the rule year-in and year-out. Government spending has thus been destabilizing rather than stabilizing, as the latter would require the government to operate its budget at a surplus during the strong part of the economic cycle.

Another myth that has recently been shattered is that the government can add employees without regard to the economy and its financial situation. States and municipalities with unbalanced budgets can still hire more employees, as long as their credit ratings justify their borrowing enough to make up for the deficit created. Eventually, lenders will refuse to finance irresponsible management by public entities. With its power to print money to pay its bills, the federal government can postpone the day of reckoning longer than states and municipalities. However, it must eventually become more financially responsible if we are to avoid economic collapse and possibly a revolution.

The Economic Picture Ahead

Meanwhile, we can expect economic and financial problems to continue, affecting us all. In 1979, there were about 200,000 bankruptcies, exceeded only by the recession year of 1975 when 224,000 were reported. For comparison purposes, the number was 178,000 in 1970, up from 98,000 in 1960, which in turn was an increase over only 25,000 in 1950. Nor are individuals the only cases. Reliable figures are not available on how many small businesses go broke, since many will sell out, merge, or simply cease operations instead of going through bankruptcy.

Large companies have not been immune to the problem of bankruptcy, either, as indicated by the financial collapse of the Penn Central Railroad and more recently of W. T. Grant Co. Other large companies have been rumored to be near bankruptcy, but have been rescued by special government action, or behind-the-scenes action by our banking authorities. The giant Chrysler Corporation is our most recent example.

Perhaps most disturbing has been the financial disaster that has overcome entire industries, such as the Real Estate Investment Trusts. While this is not a well-known industry to the average individual, its collapse has had extremely negative effects on our building industry and even the banking system itself. Governments have not been immune, with New York City appearing as perennial candidate for "Bankrupt of the Year." Among the developed nations, Italy has been a leader in the race toward bankruptcy, with Great Britain a major competitor at times. The underdeveloped countries have many entrants in the race, with many now surviving only through the grace of the creditor nations.

The Effects on Individuals

The average individual may feel it hard to sympathize with the problems of major corporations or cities such as New York. Unfortunately, this is somewhat like the short-sighted view of the sailor lying in his bunk who was told by an agitated companion that the ship was sinking. His reply was "So what? It's not my ship." As individuals, we are caught up in the problems besetting our government, our cities, and our corporations, whether we like it or not. When industry has financial problems, it cannot expand capacity. On the one hand, this reduces employment opportunities. On the other hand, it leads to shortages of various products, adding to inflationary pressures. Financial problems at the government level bring about lost job opportunities, higher taxes, and a lower standard of living.

These trends are already well underway. First, we have experienced escalating inflation, which reduces our real standard of living. The following table illustrates the ups and downs that have occurred in the past decade, with a continuing downward trend in spendable income.

Year	Average Weekly Earnings	Cost of Living Index	Weekly Earnings Adjusted For Decline In Dollar	Spendable Average Weekly Earnings for Worker with 3 Dependents	
				In Current Dollars	In 1967 Dollars
1979 *(est.)*	219.35	215.0	102.00	194.39	92.00
1978	203.70	195.4	104.30	180.71	92.53
1977	189.00	181.5	104.13	169.93	93.63
1976	175.45	170.5	102.90	155.87	91.42
1975	163.53	161.2	101.15	145.65	90.35
1974	154.76	147.7	104.78	134.61	91.14
1973	145.39	133.1	109.23	127.38	95.70
1972	139.60	125.3	109.76	121.68	97.11
1971	127.31	121.3	104.95	112.43	92.69
1970	119.83	116.3	103.04	104.90	90.20
1969	114.61	109.8	104.38	99.99	91.07
1968	107.73	104.2	103.39	95.28	91.44
1967	101.84	100.0	101.84	90.86	90.86

More Is Less

Some individuals who earn more money today than they did a few years ago may not be aware at first that their real income has been reduced. They have also been encouraged by prevailing "easy credit" policies to maintain high standards of living by going deeper into debt. But this is temporary relief. The cost of carrying this debt takes an increasing share of personal income, especially since it is not only the *debt* that rises, but the *interest rate* on each dollar of debt as inflation increases.

During the inflationary spiral of the last decade, the level of interest rates almost tripled, raising the cost of borrowing for all purposes. The combination of rising building costs and the approximate tripling of interest rates on mortgages has priced the average American out of the single-family dwelling market.

It's easy to see why even the person with a regular income has financial troubles during inflationary times. But the greatest burden falls on the individual who loses the job as a result of uncontrolled inflation.

When houses are priced out of the reach of most potential buyers, many construction workers must find other work or enter the ranks of the unemployed. The company or even the city facing bankruptcy is not likely to provide new employment opportunities, and may have been dismissing even long-term employees.

The rising unemployment rate in recent years is alarming, particularly during periods when inflation and recession occur simultaneously. Even in prolonged periods of business expansion, unemployment has stayed well above previous periods of prosperity.

What Needs to Be Done

We see no easy or early solution to the problems we have mentioned. A good case can be made that the problems will continue to escalate until our present economic system is destroyed. Before that happens, however, it is our hope that enough citizens will realize that the fundamental source of inflation is *uncontrolled government spending and interference with the private economy.* We believe that a highly limited government and a free-market economy based on the supremacy of individual rights are the best ultimate solutions.

Peter Drucker, who is a leading management consultant, attributes the greater productivity and effectiveness of business enterprises (as compared to government organizations) to the fact that business must adapt to the pressures of the marketplace and the realities of profit and loss. Governments have no such objective measurement of performance. Drucker has said:

> *"Businessmen are just as sentimental about yesterday as bureaucrats. They are just as reluctant to abandon anything. They are just as likely to respond to the failure of a product or program by doubling the efforts invested in it. But they are, fortunately, unable to indulge freely in their predilections. They stand under an objective discipline of the market. They have an objective outside measurement, profitability."*[1]

The individual who has been alerted to these basic economic problems has a better chance of survival than one who is unaware. The matter is particularly difficult, as we have a combination of inflation and depression and contraction. Therefore, we must maintain enough financial flexibility to survive the contraction periods. It is instructive to note that periods of financial irresponsibility and runaway inflation have typically been terminated by financial collapse and waves of bankruptcy. In effect, the bankruptcies serve the purpose of giving the individuals, companies, and the economy a fresh start. Capital is also released for use in more productive ways.

What Bankruptcy Means

In the Introduction, we referred to the question of whether bankruptcy is a sign of dishonesty, stupidity, or irresponsibility. The evidence we have reviewed supports the view that any individual can be a victim of economic circumstances beyond his/her control. One study of bankrupt persons showed that in at least half of the cases, the bankruptcy was beyond the individual's control, being due to reduced income, unexpected medical expenses, marital troubles, or personal liability suits.

[1]Drucker, Peter, *The Age of Discontinuity*, Harper & Row, 1969.

One quarter of the bankruptcies involved lack of prudent financial management. Only 13% involved deliberate irresponsibility toward debt repayment. The bankruptcy laws do not protect a debtor when fraud is involved, as we shall see later. Instead, our bankruptcy laws are based on the concept that every *honest* person deserves a fresh start.

How Individuals Help Create Their Financial Problems

A dismal picture has been presented of the economic and financial world in which we live. But many people will survive and even prosper in spite of tough times. The president of a successful company in a regulated industry known for many failures was asked the secret of his success. He pointed out first that his company was efficiently operated, with 15% profit margins as compared to 5% for its competitors. During good times, the company was still profitable, while many competitive companies were unprofitable and screaming to the regulators for rate relief. During these times, the successful company was able to buy up properties of its competitors at bargain rates, and was able to continue growing in this manner.

What has this to do with individuals? In many ways each of us is a money-making business, whether we are self-employed or not. We have income and expenses, assets and liabilities. It is a well-known fact that most small businesses go broke within a few years after being started, and a major contributing factor has been that the owners did not fully understand financial management.

Benefits of a Strong Financial Position

An individual who has a strong financial position is always able to take advantage of bargains that inevitably develop during any boom and bust cycle. When they do buy on credit, these people typically can get lower interest rates than the financially-burdened can. At times, it may be much cheaper to buy a home than to rent, and the financially-strong individuals can take advantage of the situation. The examples are endless.

The two financial statements that each successful business person must master are the Income Statement and the Balance Sheet. The Income Statement records the income and expenses of the business. The Balance Sheet is the statement of assets and liabilities of the business. The two statements are closely related, as the Balance Sheet will tend to improve when the Income Statement is favorable. Conversely, a strong Balance Sheet also helps the Income Statement as assets help create income, and liabilities create expenses.

Your Personal Financial Picture

Each individual also has an Income Statement and Balance Sheet, although we might not recognize them as such. The Income Statement is the family budget. It begins with the family's gross income, from which various expenses must be deducted. Ideally, if income exceeds expenses, the residue is put into savings, which serves to build up the family's financial position. When expenses exceed income, the difference can temporarily be made up by borrowing or buying on credit. But we must stress the temporary nature of this adjustment. Below is an illustration of an effective budget format. The figures are arbitrary.

BUDGET

Income	
Salaries, excluding irregular overtime	$ 9,100
Interest or other regular income	100
Add temporary income	1,800
Gross Income	**$11,000**

Expenses	
Reserve for emergencies	800
Food	2,700
Rent	2,400
Utilities	700
Furniture	400
Clothing	600
Medical	700
Insurance	600
Education	400
Transportation	600
Total Expenses	$ 9,900
Available for Savings or Debt Repayment	**$ 1,100**

Special features of this budget deserve attention. Note that income is separated into regular and temporary. A common mistake of many couples is to base their budget on two salaries, even when one spouse's income is known to be temporary. This occurs in the case of a spouse returning to school or college to finish an education, or the starting of a family where the wife intends to take time off from work for some time after childbirth. If the temporary income is not used for savings or for reducing debt, it can still be used for cash purchases of items not part of the regular weekly budget.

A second feature of the budget is debt repayment being segregated from current cash expenditures. Many of the expense items (such as furniture) are discretionary at the time of purchase. Once the purchase is made on credit, however, the payments are no longer discretionary. It is a good rule to pay cash for such items, or finance them over a short period of time. In contrast, a long-term mortgage on a home may be completely justified, as it takes the place of rent which would have to be paid otherwise. Similarly, payments on a car substitute for taxi and bus fare. Typically, debt repayments should not exceed 15% of the budget, excluding mortgage payments.

Contingency Planning

One final item deserves special attention. Many budgets survive until the unexpected happens. No provision has been made for dental or medical emergencies, car repairs, etc. Obviously these problems will occur eventually, so some preparation is necessary. That is why a reserve for emergencies heads the list of expenses in our sample budget.

It is difficult to say that expenses in any one area are too high, as the circumstances of each household vary widely. It is possible, however, to make comparisons of the ways in which typical American families spend their money, based on figures from the Department of Labor. In August, 1978, household income figures used in the study were $18,622, up 8.9% from a year previously. In the table to follow, this median income household is compared with two other levels, one with higher income of $27,420 and one with lower income of $11,546. The statistics are for an urban family of four, with the primary wage earner being a 38-year-old male.

	Low	Median	High
Total Income	$11,546	$18,622	$27,420
Total Family Consumption	9,371	14,000	19,225
Food	3,574	4,609	5,806
Housing	2,233	4,182	6,345
Transportation	856	1,572	2,043
Clothing	847	1,209	1,768
Personal Care	301	403	570
Medical Care	1,065	1,070	1,116
Other Family Consumption	515	956	1,578
Other Items	502	810	1,365
Taxes and Deductions	1,654	3,811	6,830
Social Security	719	1,073	1,091
Personal Income Tax	935	2,738	5,739

As would be expected, the amount of money spent on the basic necessities rises at a slower rate than the increase in income. As the age of the head of the family increases, the amount spent on medical expenses rises, while the amount spent on other items tends to fall. Families with more children tend to spend more on food and clothing. City dwellers have higher housing costs.

The relationships can be seen better when expenditures are given as a percentage of total income.

	Expenditures as Percent of Income		
	Low	Median	High
Total Family Consumption	81.3%	55.3%	70.1%
Food	30.9	24.8	21.2
Housing	19.3	22.5	23.2
Transportation	7.5	8.5	7.4
Clothing	7.4	6.5	6.4
Personal Care	2.6	2.2	2.1
Medical Care	9.2	5.7	4.1
Other Family Consumption	4.4	5.1	5.7
Other Items	4.4	4.4	5.0
Taxes and Deductions	14.4	20.5	24.9
Social Security	6.3	5.8	4.0
Personal Income Tax	8.1	14.7	20.9

The individual who has made up a family budget can analyze what expense items, if any, are out of line with the above percentages, which can be used as broad guidelines.

A second problem may be that debt purchases have been bunched too closely together, increasing debt repayment above the danger point. Restructuring of one's debts is a major element in improving an individual's financial health.

Let us turn now to the second financial statement mentioned earlier — the Balance Sheet. The following illustration is an example.

BALANCE SHEET

Assets (Current)	
Checking Account	$ 200
Savings Account	800
Insurance Cash Value	700
Total Current Assets	$ 1,700
Fixed Assets	
House (appraised value)	$45,000
Car	2,000
Furniture	4,000
Total Fixed Assets	$51,000
Total Assets	$52,700
Liabilities	
Installment Debt	$ 2,500
Mortgage	30,000
Total Liabilities	$32,500
Net Worth (Assets less Liabilities)	$20,200

The family used in this example has a net worth of $20,200, most of which is a result of the value of the home exceeding the mortgage against it by $15,000 ($45,000 value minus $30,000 due). The latter is probably due more to inflation than to savings. In spite of this substantial net worth, the above family may have trouble meeting their expenses from current income. The Balance Sheet represents a sort of reserve which can be drawn on to a certain extent to meet the difference.

For instance, if expenses exceeded income by $100 a month, the $1,700 in current assets could be used to bridge the gap for seventeen months. The equity in the home and furniture is much more difficult to utilize, so we have segregated this into "fixed assets." The two basic problems in utilizing net worth to meet a shortage of income are:

1. Net worth is a fixed, finite amount, so this adjustment can be only temporary.

2. Net worth produces income in one form or another, so that use of net worth aggravates the problem of income shortage. For example, the savings account may produce income of $48 per year. The equity of $15,000 in the house may produce a savings in mortgage interest payments of $100 per month.

Many financially successful individuals compute their net worth each year to see if their situation is improving or declining. The person who fails to improve the Income Statement and Balance Sheet over time is in financial danger and must be especially careful.

Avoiding Involuntary Bankruptcy

The person who is financially over-extended may still be able to survive, particularly if he/she is young and has a successful career underway. The future income may be expected to rise faster than expenses, if the temptation to step up the standard of living with each raise is consciously avoided. The long-term future may be quite good, provided that he/she survives the short term. This chapter is devoted to the pitfalls we may encounter that could lead to involuntary bankruptcy in the short term.

We have mentioned that there are many contributing factors to bankruptcy, including divorce, sudden medical bills, lawsuits, and prolonged unemployment. However, an important contributing factor in many cases is the unwise use or mismanagement of credit. The problem of managing your debt load is critical to your ability to survive financial problems successfully.

First, we will review the basic arguments for and against liberal use of credit, attempting to provide the background necessary for you to decide the level of debt with which you are comfortable or safe. Second, we suggest how you might be much more selective in your use of credit agreements. Third, there is a discussion of the problems of becoming a bad credit risk, and how to avoid this. Finally, the chapter introduces the concept of making yourself more "bankrupt-proof" and avoiding certain actions that may be fraudulent and/or cause your creditors to plunge you into involuntary bankruptcy.

Using Credit as an Asset

The ability to borrow money when it is needed is a great asset which is, unfortunately, often squandered. The financially unsophisticated person will typically pay a higher price for an item if it can be bought on credit. Cash purchases are usually cheaper, even before adding interest charges to the credit purchase. Certain businesses owe their survival to the type of customer who tends to think in terms of low downpayment and low monthly payments, rather than of total price and value received.

One observer at bankruptcy proceedings has commented that the assets may be articles such as encyclopedias bought impulsively on credit, but still in their original boxes unopened. How unlikely it would have been for these families to buy these things if a significant portion of the total price had been required in cash.

Avoiding Impulse Buying

In the last few years of rampant inflation, much attention has been drawn to the avoidance of impulse buying. Homemakers have been advised to make out lists of items needed before going to the grocery store, to help avoid the temptation of buying non-essential items on impulse. Similarly, the wide-spread availability of credit cards has received considerable criticism for making the unwise use of credit too easy for the consumer.

The amount of credit available to each of us is limited, just as our cash assets are limited. There is nothing wrong with buying a set of encyclopedias for $900 worth of credit, unless it interferes with your buying something which is needed more. There is no sound reason for a family to have a $900 set of encyclopedias when it cannot afford a reliable car with which to get to work, or does not have funds for monthly rent or decent food. Yet this seems to be typical of people on whom the high-ticket item, door-to-door salespeople prey.

Determining Your Credit Limit

What is the amount of credit that you should be able to incur safely? This figure varies widely among individuals, depending on health, stability of employment, prospects for salary increases, etc. One rule of thumb is that debt repayment costs, exclusive of your mortgage, should not exceed 20% of your income.

During inflationary times, a strong argument is often heard in favor of heavy borrowing. The argument runs something like this:

> *The dollar becomes worth less every year, so why not borrow today, invest in assets which will increase in value, and pay back the debt in dollars of lower purchasing power in future years? Fortunes have been made by businesspeople following this simple principle.*

Unfortunately, this is a technique that can backfire, as many investors have discovered in recent years. Such assets as urban real estate and common stocks, not to mention bonds, have gone *down* in dollar value while the debt owned has remained the same. Meanwhile, the interest rate on debt has skyrocketed, as people who lend money realize and demand a higher interest rate during inflationary times. The fortunes made in the past by heavy use of debt were accomplished when investment returns were high and the interest rates were low. This has not been the case in recent years.

As a person gets deeper into debt, the cost of borrowing rises sharply. A prime customer of a bank may be able to borrow at 10% interest. If this person's debt load were heavier, he/she might have to pay 18% interest to a finance company. As the debt load becomes extreme, the friendly neighborhood loan shark who charges usurious rates might be the last resort. Or the person may be forced to buy from merchants who don't violate usury laws directly, but who do so indirectly by charging higher prices for their merchandise, impose extra fees, or require the customer to purchase expensive credit insurance. A heavy debt load is a burden during inflationary times, not an asset.

Strategic use of debt, however, can be a great advantage. In our modern "stop-and-go" economy, interest rates will drop during the recession phase to levels below those which would be justified by the inflation rate. One investment rule of thumb is that interest rates tend to approximate 3% plus the expected rate of inflation. If inflation was expected to be 6%, then interest rates would trend toward 9% on low-risk investments. During the recession period, however, actual rates may be well below that level temporarily. This is the ideal time for borrowing if it is to be done. At this time, many items will also have declined in price temporarily. Downpayments and terms on major purchases, such as homes, will be very favorable compared to at other times in the business cycle.

Shopping Around

The smart borrower will not only take advantage of the business cycle to do personal borrowing on advantageous terms, but will shop for loans just as he/she shops for goods. Bank rates will normally be lower than those offered by finance companies, but interest rates will also vary among banking institutions. The rates for different types of loans will also vary, as can be seen when we compare interest rates on mortgages to installment credit rates of 18% to 36%.

The astute borrower, then, is one who would not buy for cash. Major items are purchased when prices and/or interest rates are low due to a slow down in the economy, and the best rates are shopped for.

The borrower who is already over-extended is not in a strategic position to take advantage of these opportunities. Unable to buy for cash or credit from the more conservative lenders, such borrowers must turn to high risk lenders who charge higher interest rates to compensate for the additional risk they accept.

These high risk lenders have often been a source of sorrow to unwary borrowers who may have signed contracts they did not fully understand.

What to Look For In Contracts

Credit counselors have urged that before signing contracts, borrowers should:

1. Know what interest rate is being charged. Under the Truth-in-Lending legislation, the rate must be given in the contract. In previous practice, the interest rate in installment credit was often stated at only about half the actual rate.*
2. Read the entire contract before signing it. Make certain that all blank spaces are filled in or crossed out. Make sure that the charges are itemized. Be certain that all promises made by the salesperson are in writing within the contract. Obtain a copy of the contract. Check the specifics of any guarantees, and question any items which you do not understand.

The chances of being deceived or misled are great. A salesperson may promise something different from what the written contract states, but the written contract is all that counts should a dispute arise.

One acquaintance told me of being asked by a furniture dealer to sign a paper saying a piece of furniture, which had just been ordered minutes before, had been received in good condition. In another incident, his wife signed a contract for the purchase of a mattress and discovered later that she had signed a contract for the purchase of both mattress and box springs, even though the latter had not even been discussed.

*A 12% interest rate might have been stated on a $1,000 loan, based on annual interest of $120 per year. This method is grossly misleading, since it ignores that the average money borrowed would be only about $500.

Read The Fine Print

Simply by reading the contract, the average consumer could have avoided these difficulties. Numerous pitfalls lurk in the fine print, however, and their avoidance requires some elementary legal knowledge. Debtors have often been tripped up on the following:

1. **Late Payment Clause** How late can the payment be made, without incurring a late charge? How much is the late charge?
2. **Acceleration of Payments** This is a very dangerous clause which states that if the borrower fails to make any payment when it is due, the creditor has the right to accelerate the payments and declare them due immediately. In some cases, the payments may be accelerated because the borrower is not taking good care of the property, or even because the property is taken out of state without permission of the creditor.
3. **Title Retention** This clause provides that the creditor owns the property until all payments, including late charges, have been paid.
4. **Add-on Purchases** This situation develops when a customer buys a new item on credit from a store before other items from the same store have been paid for. A new contract is signed for the new item on credit, plus the remaining balance on the older items. Should the borrower default, he/she loses not only the newly-purchased items, but also the older ones which were largely paid for.
5. **Deficiency Balances** Many people unable to keep up payments on a purchase end up with the article being repossessed. The transaction doesn't end there, however, as many debtors might expect. If the article is then resold for less than the balance owed, the original purchaser is still responsible for the deficiency balance.

6. **Holder in Due Course** This clause arises when the installment buyer also signs a negotiable promissory note along with the installment contract. A negotiable note can be sold to a third party, who becomes a "holder in due course." What happens when the seller fails to live up to the company's end of the contract? The debtor is still obligated to pay the third party who bought the promissory note! The recent consumer protection acts attempt to limit these abuses.
7. **Waiver of Defense** This is a clause which states that the buyer agrees that should he/she have a claim against the seller, that claim will not be used against any finance company that buys the contract. (This is a variation of #6, but more explicit.)
8. **Wage Assignment** The borrower assigns a certain portion of wages to making payment to the creditor. If the borrower falls behind in payments, the creditor can obligate the employer to deduct the specific amount.

As you can see from these clauses found in installment contracts, the signing of a sales contract should not be a casual undertaking. Anyone who has accumulated a great deal of debt is undoubtedly vulnerable to one or a number of the above clauses. These are similar to traps ready to be sprung once the borrower establishes a poor credit record or appears to be a bad credit risk.

How do you avoid being classified as a bad credit risk? Unfortunately, many factors in a person's credit rating may be beyond his/her direct control. Business executives and accountants tend to be regarded as good credit risks, while people involved in common labor or menial occupations tend to rank as less favorable credit risks. However, some people tend to reduce their ratings far below what they would be otherwise by making several errors.

What to do First

For example, when a payment is going to be delayed, notify the creditor ahead of time if possible. Ideally, make a partial payment rather than no payment at all. A credit manager will worry less if your balance is being gradually reduced than if the balance remains unchanged. It is better not to begin patronizing a competitor, as the initial lender will probably be more tolerant if you are still an active customer. Finally, it is better to avoid making late payments to a number of creditors. Small payments should be made on time, rather than establishing a reputation of being late on all accounts.

Once you become a bad credit risk, you have entered the danger zone of involuntary bankruptcy. If a creditor knows that you are in a bad financial situation, the creditor may try to get a headstart on other creditors by trying to collect first. An involuntary bankruptcy case can be initiated by one to three creditors, depending upon the amount of your obligations. Aggregate dollar amount of claims must be at least $5,000 more than the value of any item on your property securing those claims. Under the old bankruptcy law, it was necessary to commit an act of bankruptcy to bring about involuntary bankruptcy proceedings. Now the court considers whether a debtor is unable to pay debts as they become due, or if a custodian was appointed to take charge of the debtor's property.

Even if you eventually have to declare voluntary bankruptcy, there are important advantages to this over the involuntary bankruptcy situation. With extra time at your disposal, you can take legal steps to retain a greater portion of your assets, as will be seen in the chapter on voluntary bankruptcy.

New Forms of Protection

With the passage of the new bankruptcy laws, you have some important protection against being brought into involuntary bankruptcy. Farmers or ranchers are protected, due to the uncertain nature of their earnings. Also, if the court dismisses a petition under this section, other than with consent of all petitioners and you, the court may grant judgement against the petitioners for costs, attorneys' fees, or any damages caused by taking possession of your property.

Debt Readjustment Plan (Chapter 13) for Individual With Regular Income

Many individuals have reasonably good financial prospects, provided they can survive the short-term. The major problem of debt can often be solved by lengthening payment time.

It is a good sound principle in corporate finance to sell on favorable finance terms. The automobile and home building industries owe much of their past growth to the simple technique of enabling consumers to pay for their products over longer periods of time.

Finance companies take advantage of this principle by urging consumers with large monthly debt repayments to apply for debt consolidation loans. A longer debt repayment period at a reduced single payment can permit the retirement of debt over a longer period of time. Unfortunately, many debtors, encouraged by the lower monthly payment, immediately go further into debt, so that the relief is only temporary. Also, the new debt consolidation loan may have a very high interest rate, so that most of the monthly payment goes to pay interest rather than the principle.

Changes in Chapter 13

An alternative to the above situation is protection of the debtor under Chapter 13 of the Bankruptcy Law. This was known as the *Wage Earner's Plan* and was once available only to a person whose principal income was from wages, salaries, or commissions. However, it is now available to individuals with income sufficiently regular to enable them to make payments under a Chapter 13 plan. This would include investment income, Social Security, pensions, or income from self-employment. Under the old law, a small business owner could not file under Chapter 13. This is no longer the case.

With Chapter 13, debts are not wiped out, but they can be settled in some cases at less than the full amount. Generally, debts are stretched out over thirty-six months, but this can be extended to five years with court approval. Technically the person is not a bankruptcy case, and the petition which is filed refers to him/her as a debtor. Under the old law, debts were to be paid from future income; but under the new law, payments can also be made from partial liquidation of assets. This is in contrast to bankruptcy proceedings where a person's assets, with certain important exceptions, will be liquidated to pay debts to the extent possible from the proceeds.

Disadvantages

The use of the wage earner's plan instead of bankruptcy has had its opponents and its defenders. The advantage of the straight bankruptcy route is that a person gets a fresh start and is relieved of the burden of most obligations. In contrast, the thirty-six month repayment period in the wage earner's plan is an extended time during which the debtor's standard of living will be restricted by debt repayment. Interestingly, wage earner plans are most commonly used in rural or small town communities where bankruptcy still has a strongly negative image. (We feel this negative image is unjustified, of course.) The difficulty of surviving the long period of restraint is evidenced by the fact that over half of the Chapter 13 cases fail because the debtor does not keep up payments. Surveys have shown that a large percentage of Chapter 13 debtors have had previous experience with either straight bankruptcy or a wage earner plan.

Advantages

Nevertheless, the wage earner's plan does have undeniably important advantages. First, it may be more effective in reforming debtors than some critics believe. One survey showed that only 38% of first-time participants in a wage earner's plan successfully completed the plan, whereas the percentage jumped to over 65% for individuals filing for a second time or more. From the debtor's viewpoint, he/she gains protection from creditor harrassment. Once a petition for relief is filed, a court order may be sent to each creditor restricting them from garnishing wages or attaching assets. Exorbitant interest and credit charges will be disallowed. Certain disputed claims may be dismissed. It forces debtors to learn elementary budgeting and to exercise restraint in spending.

Strangely enough, the debtor electing the wage earner plan could probably get more relief than is usually asked for. The debtor's plan usually provides for payments of debts at 100% on the dollar, asking only for an extension of time to pay the debts. However, the debtor can petition for a plan that pays considerably less than 100% for each dollar of debt, in which case the plan is called a "composition" of the debts. Whether creditors will agree to such a plan depends on the bargaining power of the debtor. If the debtor has no assets, or most of the assets would be retained in spite of bankruptcy, the creditors may very well prefer accepting a composition rather than getting nothing as a result of straight bankruptcy.

How to Begin

The first step in proceeding in the debtor's plan is for the debtor to develop a plan for paying debts, to be submitted to the Court. The table on the following page is the type of information which is included in filing your petition.

Note that estimated future monthly expenses of the family do not include debts to be paid under the plan, as these are included in the last item on the budget (d), Total amount to be paid each month under the plan. However, payments on secured debts not covered by the plan would be listed under expenses. The new law greatly strengthens the debtor's position in negotiation with creditors.

EXAMPLE OF A HOUSEHOLD BUDGET

(A) Give estimated average future monthly income for each spouse whether single or joint petition is filed unless spouses are separated and a single petition is filed.

(1) Husband's monthly take-home pay	$500
(2) Wife's monthly take-home pay	300
(3) Other monthly income (specify)	____
Total	$800

(B) Give estimated average future monthly expenses of family (not including debts to be paid under plan), consisting of:

(1) Rent or home mortgage payment (include lot rental for trailer)	$200
(2) Utilities (Electricity $30.00 Heat $50.00 Water $10.00 Telephone $10.00)	100
(3) Food	250
(4) Clothing	20
(5) Laundry and cleaning	20
(6) Newspapers, periodicals, and books (including school books)	10
(7) Medical and drug expenses	10
(8) Insurance (not deducted from wages): (a) Auto $20.00 (b) Other $10.00...........	30
(9) Transportation (not including auto payments to be paid under plan)....................	—
(10) Recreation.............................	20
(11) Club and union dues (not deducted from wages)	—

	(12) Taxes (not deducted from wages)	—
	(13) Alimony, maintenance, or support payments ...	—
	(14) Other payments for support of dependents not living at home	—
	(15) Other (specify)	____
	Total	$660
(C)	Excess of estimated future monthly income (last line of Item (A) above)	$140
(D)	**Total amount to be paid each month under plan....**	**$120**

If monthly income exceeds monthly expenses, the difference is available for debt repayment. To calculate this, all debts covered by the plan are added. The total debt figure is then increased by 10% to allow for estimated court costs, and this figure is divided by 36 — the typical period in months selected for debt repayment. This figure is compared with the one in item (C), excess of estimated future monthly income over estimated future expenses. If item (C), income after expenses, is larger than item (D), the amount to be paid each month, the plan can succeed.

If income after expenses is not greater than the figure for debt repayment, reduce the debt repayment figure by various percentages. This could range to as much as 80% or 90% or as little as 10% or 20%, depending on how much of a reduction is necessary to permit income after expenses to cover debt repayment.

It is vitally important to keep the *same* percentage of proposed debt reduction for *all* creditors of the same class. With the reduced amount, this plan can then be proposed to creditors. If they do not accept the plan, serious considerations can then be given to voluntary bankruptcy. When you advise your creditors that you wish to pay your debts in full, or as large a percentage as you can possibly handle, and that your alternative is bankruptcy, the tendency is often for them to accept the offer.

Creditors of the same class must receive equal treatment in the plan. For example, if one unsecured creditor is to be paid 80¢ on the dollar, then all are to be treated that way. *Secured creditors* have to be negotiated separately, and they may be able to enforce their claims completely since they can repossess property covered by the debt. Should the value of the property be worth less than the amount of the debt, however, the debtor is in an excellent position to negotiate with even the secured creditor. The amount by which a secured creditor's claim exceeds the "fair" value of his collateral is includable only as part of the unsecured claim. This portion of the claim may receive less than 100¢ on the dollar. The plan may also provide for payment of "priority" claims. These might include taxes or wages due an employee of the debtor.

Requirements for Approval

In order for the court to confirm the plan, it must comply with Chapter 13 of the Act, required fees must be paid. Plans must have been proposed in good faith and not by any means forbidden by law. Under the plan, unsecured creditors must receive not less than they would in straight bankruptcy. Secured creditors either must have accepted the plan, received the property covered by the claim, or retained their liens and will receive property not less than the amount of such claim. Confirmation will also depend on the ability of the debtor to make all payments under the plan.

A set of forms which can be used in filing for Chapter 13 can be purchased from Julius Blumberg, Inc., 66 White Street, New York, New York, 10013. Write to them for their most current order booklet and costs. A set would include the following:

1. Instruction sheet
2. Original Petition Under Chapter 13
3. Statement of Affairs
4. Plan

5. Creditors List
6. Worksheets
7. Heavy-duty envelopes and covers

The Petition under Chapter 13 is largely self-explanatory, and a facsimile follows. This, and all other forms in this book, were reproduced by permission of Julius Blumberg, Inc.

UNITED STATES BANKRUPTCY COURT FOR THE DISTRICT OF Case No.

In re

CHAPTER 13

Debtor Include here all names used by debtor within last 6 years.

(If this form is used for joint petitioners wherever the word "petitioner" or words referring to petitioners are used they shall be read as if in the plural.)

VOLUNTARY CASE: DEBTOR'S *JOINT* PETITION[1]

1. Petitioner's post-office address is

2. Petitioner has ☐ resided within this district for the preceding 180 days.
☐ had his*(her)* domicile within this district for the preceding 180 days.
☐ had his*(her)* principal place of business within this district for the preceding 180 days.
☐ resided or been domiciled or had his*(her)* principal place of business within this district for a longer portion of the preceding 180 days than in any other district.

3. Petitioner is qualified to file this petition and is entitled to the benefits of title 11, United States Code as a voluntary debtor.

4. ☐ A copy of petitioner's proposed plan, dated 19 is attached.
☐ Petitioner intends to file a plan pursuant to chapter 13 of title 11, United States Code.

Wherefore, petitioner prays for relief in accordance with chapter 13 of title 11, United States Code.

Petitioner(s) signs if not represented by attorney

Signed:..
Attorney for Petitioner

Address:..
....

....
Petitioner

....
Petitioner

DECLARATION[2]

INDIVIDUAL: I, the petitioner named in the foregoing petition, certify under penalty of perjury that the foregoing is true and correct.

JOINT INDIVIDUALS: We, and the petitioners named in the foregoing petition, certify under penalty of perjury that the foregoing is true and correct.

Executed on 19 Signature:..
Petitioner

....
Petitioner

Form Nos. 1 & 2 combined & 5, chapter 13, Voluntary case: debtor's petition individual, joint, 10-79.

1 The filing of a joint petition is authorized by 11 U.S.C. §302.
2 The unsworn declaration conforms with Public Law 94-550, 90 Stat. 2534, 28 U.S.C. §1746 (1976) which permits the declaration to be made in the form indicated with the same force and effect as a sworn statement.

3070 Form Nos. 1, 2 & 5, chapter 13

© 1979 JULIUS BLUMBERG, INC.

The second part of the form set is a six-page Statement of Affairs which requests the following information:

1. Name and residence
2. Occupation and income
3. Dependents
4. Budget (reproduced earlier in this chapter)
5. Payment of attorney
6. Tax refunds
7. Bank accounts and Safe Deposit Boxes
8. Prior bankruptcy
9. Foreclosures, Executions, and Attachments
10. Repossessions and Returns
11. Debts
12. Co-debtors
13. Property

At the end of the statement, there is a space for the petitioner to sign in the presence of a Notary Public. The Statement of Affairs is similar to the one filed for bankruptcy, and instructions for completing this form are covered in Chapter 6.

In addition to the Petition under Chapter 13 and the Statement of Affairs, a form entitled "Chapter 13 Plan" must be completed. This plan is based primarily on the budget information included in the Statement of Affairs, and a copy of the form entitled "Chapter 13 Plan" must be completed. This plan is based primarily on the budget information included in the Statement of Affairs, and a copy of the form Chapter 13 Plan follows.

UNITED STATES BANKRUPTCY COURT FOR THE DISTRICT OF Case No.

In re

Debtor, Soc. Sec. No.
[Include here all names used by debtor within last 6 years.]

CHAPTER 13
PLAN

(If this form is used by joint debtors wherever the word "debtor" or words referring to debtor are used they shall be read as if in the plural.)

1. The future earnings of the debtor are submitted to the supervision and control of the trustee and the *debtor — debtor's employer* shall pay to the trustee the sum of $ *weekly — bi-weekly — semi-monthly — monthly.*

2. From the payments so received, the trustee shall make disbursements as follows:
(a) The priority payments required by 11 U.S.C. §507.
(b) After the above payments, dividends to secured creditors whose claims are duly proved and allowed as follows:

(c) *Subsequent to — pro rata with* dividends to secured creditors, dividends to unsecured creditors whose claims are duly proved and allowed as follows:

3. The following executory contracts of the debtor are rejected:

Title to the debtor's property shall revest in the debtor *on confirmation of a plan — upon dismissal of the case after confirmation pursuant to 11 U.S.C. §1329 — upon closing of the case pursuant to 11 U.S.C. §350.*

Dated: .... *Debtor* .... *Debtor*

Acceptances may be mailed to........................ *Post Office Address*

Revised OF 13-6: Chapter 13 Plan, 10-79

Definitions

Two terms used in the form require some explanation. These are "priority claims" and "executory contract." For definition of priority claims, refer to the discussion in Chapter 6 regarding Schedule A-1 of the Bankruptcy forms. The term "executory contract" refers to a contract that obligates the debtor to pay in the future for some service. For example, if you have signed a contract to buy a television set but have not yet received it, you need not list the debt *except* under the section "executory contracts." Leases may also fall under this category. If an attorney is used by the petitioner, a form called "Statement of Compensation" must be submitted, signed by the attorney.

Some important differences between Chapter 13 plans and bankruptcy should be pointed out:

1. Bankruptcies are a quicker way to resolve financial problems, since Chapter 13 plans are stretched out over a period of time, typically thirty-six months.
2. Historically, a large percentage of Chapter 13 plans failed to succeed, whereas a high percentage of bankruptcy plans were completed. Under the new law, however, the likelihood of success of such plans has been greatly increased. With better ability to negotiate reduced payments of debts, the debtor is in a much better position to match available income and monthly payments. If the debtor fails to complete payments due to circumstances beyond his control, the court may still grant a discharge, provided creditors have received as much as they would have received under straight bankruptcy.
3. Chapter 13 plans are not restricted to being undertaken every six years, as is the case with bankruptcy, provided that the debtor has paid at least 70% of the debts and used his/her best efforts.
4. Chapter 13 plans look primarily to a person's future earnings to pay off debts, whereas bankruptcy looks to a person's assets. The amount of assets that a person has becomes a major factor in the decision to go this route or to choose bankruptcy.
5. The majority of Chapter 13 plans are filed by the main wage earner in the family, although income from the spouse is included in the budgeting figures. In the case of

bankruptcy, it may be advantageous for each to file for bankruptcy.

6. A Chapter 13 plan is, in most cases, easier to handle by the layperson than bankruptcy, since the latter involves more legal advice to protect assets.

Although the Chapter 13 plan is a long-term affair compared to bankruptcy, this is not altogether a disadvantage, since you have a chance to develop better ability in making budgetary and financial decisions. Typically, the plan has considerable flexibility, as trustees realize that people cannot completely live in financial straightjackets. The court assumes that there must be some extra income in excess of the required financial payments, and would probably not approve a plan that did not provide for this. A person can still buy items on credit, but the amount must not exceed his/her obvious limits. Although the time period is usually thirty-six months, extensions can be obtained when unforeseen circumstances arise.

In summary, this plan can be successful for the financially-pressed individual who just needs more time and less harrassment to work things out. It can be a much more effective plan if the individual is in a good position to get a reduction of the debts (a composition) rather than simply an extension of time to pay them. As mentioned earlier, most creditors find it more advantageous to accept reduced payments than to see a person declare bankruptcy, where the unsecured creditor typically receives very little, if anything.

Under Chapter 13 plans, the debtor is also entitled to advice and counsel from the trustee, who must assist the debtor in adjusting the plan to accommodate changing needs and circumstances. The new law protects the debtor in situations where indirect pressure has been placed against co-debtors. This applies to cases in which family or friends have co-signed debts as an accommodation to the debtor. Creditors are stayed from processing a claim against the co-debtor, unless the debt arose in the ordinary course of the debtor's business.

The new bankruptcy law has been designed to make Chapter 14 debt readjustment more attractive, relative to bankruptcy. More people are eligible to use the plan, its protective features have been improved, and the ability of creditors to oppose the plan has been reduced.

The plan is also flexible, in order to meet the debtor's changing needs.

Questions and Answers Regarding Debt Readjustment (Chapter 13)

Q. Does the court take my paycheck?

A. Generally, funds are collectible from the employee, but, if agreeable to both employer and employee, the required amount may be sent directly to the Court. In some cases, the entire paycheck may be sent to the Court, which deducts the amount required for debt repayment and sends the remainder to you.

Q. What is the average size of the Debt Readjustment plan case?

A. In the 1971 Brookings Study, the average case had $500 of assets and $2,500 of debt, payable to seven different creditors. On the surface, it would appear advantageous to use the bankruptcy route. However, a substantial amount of the above debt was probably secured debt, which would not be cancelled out without the debtor losing assets, many of which would have to be replaced. Under the new law, the average size will probably increase due to expanded coverage.

Q. Does electing the debt readjustment plan eliminate the option of declaring bankruptcy if the plan doesn't work out?

A. No. A great many Wage Earner Plans were converted into bankruptcy cases when the payment schedule could not be kept. Under the present act, the bankruptcy judge, can give the debtor a discharge, if the creditors' have received as much as they would have under a straight bankruptcy case.

Q. *What does the debt readjustment plan do to my ability to get credit?*

A. During the early part of the plan, ability to get credit will possibly be reduced somewhat, since there is the possibility that the plan will fail and, then you will declare bankruptcy. However, it is best, possibly, that credit not be so readily available, as easy credit is typically an important part of the debtor's problem. As the plan progresses and appears to be successful, your credit rating would be improved.

Bankruptcy

Up to this point, we have stressed that a knowledge of bankruptcy can be a valuable aid in avoiding the need to petition for bankruptcy.

At this point, we will consider the possibility that alternative solutions to financial problems appear to be unworkable or at least difficult. So the advantages and disadvantages of declaring bankruptcy will be considered directly.

In this chapter, we will first review the psychological and financial factors which must be considered in arriving at a decision to declare bankruptcy. We will then outline the basic strategies of preparing for bankruptcy, so that a maximum of assets can be retained. The basic procedure is then discussed, and we cover the most commonly-asked questions about bankruptcy. Preparation of the necessary forms is deferred until Chapter 6.

Declaring bankruptcy is not strictly a financial decision, but also an important psychological one. Before discussing the strategy for making yourself as bankruptcy-proof as possible, some consideration should be given to the non-financial, personal aspects of the decision.

One frequent observer of bankruptcy cases has commented on how surprising it is that many petitioners wait so long before declaring. One of the most complete academic studies devoted to bankruptcy included questionnaires that dealt with attitudes of Americans toward bankruptcy. Interviewees were asked, for example, what they would think of doing business with a person who had gone bankrupt. Approximately 26% indicated that they would be reluctant or cautious, and would prefer to do business with someone else. The interviewees were also asked how they would feel about going bankrupt themselves. Approximately 33% said they would go bankrupt only as a last resort, and another 20% indicated that they would not go bankrupt—they would rather die! Another 18% said they would feel disgraced.[1]

Bankruptcy as Relief

While these results indicate the distaste Americans have for bankruptcy, it is interesting to note that most people who have gone through it feel better for having done so. Of those interviewed, well over half said they were better off, with approximately one quarter indicating that they were much better off. When asked about their current financial position as compared to "before bankruptcy," two-thirds indicated they were better off, with half of this group saying that they were "much better off." One could conclude that bankruptcy is not nearly as negative an experience as most Americans believe. In general, the relief from burdensome debt and creditor harrassment more than offsets any feelings of failure generated by going bankrupt.

The negative feeling toward bankruptcy is stronger in rural areas and small towns, where the relationship between creditor and debtor is less impersonal than in more urban areas. The negative feeling also tends to vary, depending upon the state of the economy. During the depression of the 1930's, unemployment and underemployment were so widespread that a person's financial failures could be attributed to the economy, rather than to

[1] Stanley, David R. and Marjorie Girth, *Bankruptcy, Problems, Process, Reform*, The Brookings Institution, 1971.

his/her own personal shortcomings.[2] In recent years, the economy has once again experienced violent contractions in area after area, in spite of all the so-called economic stabilizers, such as Social Security and unemployment compensation. The fear and distrust of bankruptcy is likely to decline under present circumstances.

A review of the history of bankruptcy and a study of present bankruptcy laws would lead to the following conclusions:

1. Historically, laws which favored punishment of debtors were not only inhumane, but produced little value to the creditor while doing great harm to the debtor.

2. Problems, including financial ones, come upon everyone, and are sometimes overwhelming. In the "battle of life," anyone can get knocked down, many times, and criticism could possibly be restricted to those who don't try to get back up.

3. Many creditors deserve little sympathy if they experience some losses in bankruptcy cases. They are aware of risks and build a loss reserve into their prices. Any business that sells on credit charges interest[3] and interest rates charged on different types of debts vary with the risk involved. Interest on installment credit is sufficiently high to pay for a lot of bankruptcy losses.

4. Present bankruptcy laws do not protect the dishonest debtor, due to the many restrictions against fraud contained in the law. The feeling that being formerly bankrupt implies dishonesty is completely unwarranted.

[2] An acquaintance tells me that during the Depression, his family received a letter from the Finance Company asking, "What would your neighbors think if we sent a truck out and repossessed all your furniture?" To which his father replied, "They would think you were a bunch of S.O.B.'s." The Finance Company did, and the neighbors did.

[3] Sometimes, no interest is charged directly, but the price of goods sold is adjusted upward over what would be charged otherwise.

From an objective point of view, there is no reason to feel inadequate or dishonest because of bankruptcy. This attitude was developed in rural American in a less complex economic period, and was not even justified then. It is certainly unjustified now, as an individual's destiny is often controlled by factors beyond his/her control. These include actions of "big government," "big labor," and sometimes "big business."

Turning from the psychological to the financial side, the decision to go bankrupt should not ignore the possibility that the Chapter 13 plan may be more attractive as an alternative. This might be true if debts could be paid off comfortably over a three-year period, but only after rearranging assets and liabilities so as to salvage as much as possible.

Debts You Will Still Have to Pay

First, there are some debts which are not discharged by bankruptcy, including the following:

1. Taxes of the United States, the state, county, district, municipality in which the bankrupt resides, not more than three years old.
2. Liabilities for obtaining property by false pretenses or false representations.
3. Alimony and child support.
4. Debts which are not listed on the schedules.
5. Liabilities for malicious injuries to the person or property of another.

The Bankruptcy Act prescribes a certain order of payment of the several classes of creditors out of the net amount of property left. There is a priority to the order in which assets are distributed. To be dealt with first are the segregation of property belonging to adverse claimants, secured creditors, exemptions, and the payment of expenses of the individual sales.

The order of priority is as follows:

1. Administrative expenses.
2. Wages and other compensation to wage-earners, earned within three months before bankruptcy.
3. Taxes.
4. Debts owning to any person entitled to priority.

Secured Debts

Another class of debts would be secured claims, and these require special attention during bankruptcy proceedings. A secured debt is one for which the creditor holds property that insures that the debt will be paid. For instance, when you get a loan for a car, the creditor often holds the title until the loan is paid off. Should you default, the creditor may come and repossess your car, and they hold the title. Much consumer installment credit is in this category, as well. The seller does not retain the property, but retains the right to repossess it if the buyer defaults. If the value of the security is more than the debt, the court will turn it over to the creditor. To the extent that the debt exceeds the value of the article, this excess will be recognized by the court but only as an unsecured debt.

All other debts are unsecured. These bear the bulk of losses during bankruptcy.

Prior to going bankrupt, the debtor typically has money to pay only part of the bills. If the choice is between paying against an unsecured debt or against debts which will not be discharged, *it is to the debtor's advantage to favor the latter claims.* In the case of secured property where the debt is greater than the value of the security, the article will be repossessed. Often however, the debtor can retain the item by making a new contract at a new price approximating resale value after the bankruptcy. *After bankruptcy, the debtor should not make any payment on old contracts, as this could revive the debts!*

Exempt Property

Prior to bankruptcy, the debtor should concentrate on paying bills for those items which can be retained after bankruptcy. An "exempt" item or asset is property which can be retained after bankruptcy, being exempt from seizure to satisfy debts, and does not have to be surrendered to the bankruptcy courts for payment of creditors. However, if the exempt item is obtained by incurring a debt, its exempt status does not prevent its being recovered by the seller.

Specific exemptions are partly determined by state law, and these vary widely. They usually include such items as apparel, working tools, home furnishings, domestic animals, life insurance, and salary and wages up to a limit.

The amount of the exemptions can vary from a few thousand dollars to fifty thousand dollars and more, depending on the state of residence. One advisor in bankruptcy cases has even suggested that a person with considerable assets who is considering bankruptcy relocate to a state with favorable exemption treatment. Since residency is determined by the location where the debtor has spent the greater part of six months, it would only take three months and one day to satisfy the residency requirements. For details on state exemptions, refer to the Appendix.

New Changes in the Law

In view of the wide discrepancy between states in regard to "exempt" assets, the new Federal Bankruptcy Law gave the debtor a choice between using the exemptions specified by his/her state or the exemptions included in the Federal Bankruptcy Code. The states may pass laws that prohibit the use of the federal exemptions, which would defeat one of the major purposes of the new Bankruptcy Code. However, it is likely that states passing such laws would be under pressure to liberalize the amount of assets protected under state law.

Ohio is one of the first states to liberalize their exemptions to be more in line with federal ones. The following table illustrates Ohio state exemptions before and after October 1, 1979, along with the federal exemptions. It should be noted, however, that the debtor must use either federal or state, and cannot pick out the best of both.

	Exemptions under Federal Bankruptcy Code 10/1/79	Exemptions under Ohio statute prior to 10/1/79	Exemptions under Ohio statute effective 10/1/79
Homestead	$7,500	$1,000	$5,000
Motor Vehicle	$1,200	None unless claimed as necessary to profession, trade, or business.	$1,000
Personal Property	All household furnishings, goods, clothes, books, etc. for personal or family use not to exceed $200 in any particular item.	All clothes of family, 2 stoves, plus fuel, $600 in livestock or furnishings and $150 in family provisions may be claimed by head of household. $300 in clothes and $300 in tools of trade may be claimed by others.	Wearing apparel, beds, not to exceed $200 in any particular item. One cooking stove and one refrigerator, not to exceed $300 each.
Personal Jewelry	$500	None.	Jewelry not to exceed $400 in any particular item.
Other Property	$400 in any property plus unused portion of homestead exemption.	None.	$400 in money.
Tools of Trade	$750	$600	$750
Professionally Prescribed Health Aids	All health aids for debtor and dependents	None.	All.

Other federal exemptions include:

1. Unmatured life insurance
2. Social Security, unemployment compensation, welfare payments, veteran's disability
3. Alimony, support, and maintenance
4. Pension or profit-sharing benefits
5. Wrongful death payments

The importance of exempt assets to the bankrupt individual can hardly be overemphasized. They offer the base upon which to rebuild one's financial status. Any person considering bankruptcy should put as much of his/her assets in these areas as possible. This will, in part, consist of paying bills on exempt items where money is owed against them. In other cases, a simple switch of funds from a checking account into a Federal Savings & Loan (in some states) or into an insurance policy with cash value (exempt in most states) or the simple purchase of an exempt article will be a strategic move.

Protecting Your Home Through Homesteading

Many individual's major asset is the equity in their homes. The best protection for this asset is "homesteading" it. Homesteading prevents the seizure of a home for any debts except those for which you have pledged the property, such as the mortgage. Here again, state laws vary widely, from $40,000 in North Dakota to none in other states. Generally, the Western states are most liberal. In some states, only a "head of the family" can qualify for homestead exemption. A married man would qualify, and usually a divorced or widowed man or woman with children under 18 years of age living at home would also qualify. Generally, the property claimed for homestead must be the principal residence of the bankrupt. Homesteading must take place before petitioning for bankruptcy. Information as to forms to be filed for homesteading can usually be obtained at the local County Clerk or County Recorder's office. Homestead exemption laws are summarized in the Appendix. Some sample homestead forms are as follows:

Declaration by husband

I, ______________________, hereby declare:

I am the head of a family, I am married, and my wife's name is ______. My family consists of my wife and ________ children.

At the time of making this declaration of homestead, I actually reside with my family on premises located in the County of ______________, State of ______________, more particularly described as follows: ________

I claim and declare the premises, with the dwelling house __________ (and outbuildings) on it, and its appurtenances, as a homestead for the joint benefit of myself and my wife and family.

______________ (No former declaration of homestead has been made by me or by my wife, either jointly or separately *or* A former declaration of homestead has been made by ______________, but it was abandoned before the execution of this declaration of homestead.)

I estimate the actual cash value of the premises to be __________ Dollars ($________).

Executed on ______________________, 19____.

(Signature)

(Acknowledgment)

Declaration by wife

I, ______________________, hereby declare:

I am a married woman, and my husband's name is ______________. My husband is the head of a family, consisting of my husband and myself ______________ (and ______________ children).

At the time of making this declaration of homestead, I actually reside on the premises described below with my husband ______________ (and family), and I claim and declare the premises, with the dwelling house ______________ (and outbuildings), and the appurtenances on it, as a homestead for the joint benefit of myself and my husband __________ (and family).

The premises on which I reside with my husband ______________ (and family) are located in the County of ______________, State of ______________, and are described as follows: ______________ *(legal description)*.

______________________ (No former declaration of homestead has been made by me or by my husband, jointly or separately *or* A former declaration of homestead has been made by ______________, but it was abandoned before the execution of this declaration of homestead.) I estimate the actual cash value of the premises to be ______________ Dollars ($ __________).

Executed on ______________, 19 ____ .

(Signature)

(Acknowledgment)

Joint declaration by husband and wife

We, ____________________ and ____________________, hereby declare:

We are husband and wife. I, ____________________ (name of husband), am the head of a family, consisting of myself and my wife ________________ (and __________ children).

At the time of making this declaration, we actually reside ____________ (with our family) on the premises described below, and we claim and declare the premises, with the dwelling house ________________ (and outbuildings) on it, and its appurtenances, as a homestead for our joint benefit ______________ (and for the benefit of our family).

The premises on which we so reside ________________ (with our family) are located in the County of ____,
State of __________________________________, and are described as follows:
________________________________ *(legal description).*

______________________________ (No former declaration of homestead has been made by either of us, jointly or separately *or* A former declaration of homestead has been made by ____________________________________, but it was abandoned before the execution of this declaration of homestead).

We estimate the actual cash value of the premises to be ______________ Dollars ($_____________).

Executed on _______________________, 19____.

(Signatures)

(Acknowledgment)

Misrepresentation

While rearranging your assets in preparation for bankruptcy, you must be extremely careful not to commit fraudulent acts. An honest error or omission without intent to defraud can be corrected. To lie or to seek to cheat in a bankruptcy proceeding is a crime, and not only would this be grounds for denial of the petition for discharge of debts, but it could also result in a fine and/or imprisonment for fraud. The debtor should not conceal, transfer, remove, destroy, or mutilate property with the intent to delay.

The destruction, falsification, or concealment of records about the bankrupt's financial condition can also be grounds for denial. Not every petitioner for bankruptcy is expected to have books, particularly individuals not in business for themselves. In most cases, salaried employees and wage earners do not have to keep books and records in order to receive a discharge. If a bankrupt has kept books, however, they should be produced.

A person may also be denied the discharge of a particular debt if he/she has obtained credit by a material false statement in writing that misrepresents financial position. This is a particularly treacherous pitfall. When applying for credit, an individual may fill out a form which has a space for listing present debts. Typically, the major debts may be listed but, due to lack of space or slip of memory, the minor debts are omitted — particularly those considered trivial. The creditor may claim that credit was issued based on the claim that this was a false statement. Even if the debtor receives general approval of the bankruptcy petition, the creditor may still sue, arguing that this debt was not dischargeable because of misrepresentation.

Protection Before the Fact

One credit counselor advises people to include a figure for miscellaneous small debts not listed specifically when filling out credit forms. If you have already bought an item based upon a credit form in which you omitted certain debts, you would be better off paying for this item before declaring bankruptcy. However, the new law is much more favorable to the debtor. A false financial statement is no longer justification for denying a general discharge.

Another temptation to avoid when contemplating bankruptcy is the salvaging of property by concealing or transferring it to others, such as friends or relatives, without receiving adequate consideration (payment). To be grounds for denial of discharge, the action must occur within twelve months immediately preceding the filing of the petition, and must be done with intent to defraud or hinder creditors. To be fraudulent, the transfer would also have to occur when you were already insolvent or made insolvent by the gift.

To avoid this pitfall, you must receive fair payment for any item you transfer to another. The payment does not have to be money, but can be another article or even cancellation of a debt which you owe to the other individual. Such a debt would have to be definite and provable. Failure to list a significant asset would probably be tolerated by the court, if it was an honest oversight and not intended to defraud. A deliberate failure to list assets would be reason to bar a discharge. The creditor has only to show that the assets existed and are not accounted for. You then have the burden of proving that the assets were not concealed, destroyed, or transferred with the intent to defraud. Your gifts during the previous twelve months to your spouse would be carefully checked. If you were not insolvent at the time of the gift, there would be no grounds for considering the transfer fradulent. However, a gift should not be made within four months of filing a petition for bankruptcy, under any circumstances.

Other grounds for denying a bankruptcy petition include a restriction on filing bankruptcy in less than six years after a previous bankruptcy, deliberate failure to obey court orders, and non-payment of filing fees.

Determining Whether You Need a Lawyer

Up to this time, we have discussed preparing for bankruptcy. If you feel you are safe from the pitfalls discussed above, you are now ready for the actual event. Probably the first question to be faced is whether a lawyer should be retained. Here a wide difference of opinion exists. One writer on the subject of bankruptcy (a non-lawyer) comments that he would approach a court of law without a lawyer with the same enthusiasm with which he would remove his own appendix. In contrast, another writer (a lawyer) takes a more balanced view. His advice would be to have a lawyer if you have substantial assets to protect, particularly a home. However, he concludes that you could do it yourself if you have no assets and you are not in business for yourself. In one extensive study of bankruptcy, the researchers concluded that clients without lawyers were at a disadvantage in negotiating with creditors.

Nevertheless, the study was extremely critical of the counselors for a very poor performance, although only 10% of the debtors were critical of their attorneys. In many cases, the amount of legal work is limited to filling out the forms and making one appearance in court, for which the bankrupt can be expected to pay a minimum of about $300.

What to Expect

The preparation of forms is covered in Chapter 6 for those interested in filing their own petitions. The information for the forms is supplied by the debtor. While they cannot give legal advice, the clerks in many courts know more about filling out forms than do most lawyers, and are willing to help. As for the appearance in court, most personal bankruptcy cases are fairly routine. A judge (called a "referee") asks questions about items contained in the petitions, and may ask questions about dispositions of property. The judge is not an opponent of the bankrupt, but is only asking questions to get the needed information. In routine cases, the first meeting can be over in far less time than an hour. For do-it-yourselfers, the first step is to obtain a set of legal forms, such as those described in Chapter 6.

A filing fee of $50 is required. If husband and wife file jointly, the fee is $60. The court determines the extent to which their estates can be consolidated.

After receiving the petition for bankruptcy, the court clerk mails to all creditors a notice of the hearing, known as the "first meeting of creditors." Typically, the time for the meeting is ten to thirty days from the date on which the petition was filed. When a bankrupt's name is called, he takes the witness stand. If the case is complex, the judge may appoint a trustee to conserve the assets, check for other assets, and make equitable distribution to the creditors. The creditors have a certain length of time to object to the debtor receiving a discharge of the debts. If a creditor does not object in writing, a hearing is held to determine the validity of the claim. After discharge, creditors are restrained from any further attempts to collect debts, and a violation of this restraint is considered contempt of court.

The Final Hearing

In a case concerning an individual, there is a final hearing, when the court has determined whether or not to grant a discharge, at which the debtor appears in person. If a discharge has been granted, the debtor receives an explanation about the discharge and is warned about reaffirmation of the dischargeable debt. Where it is determined that the debtor wishes to reaffirm a particular debt, the court reviews the agreement to see if it meets certain requirements. Agreement must be made before the grant of discharge, and it can only be rescinded within thirty days after the hearing. The debtor must have attended the meeting and have been given the warning. In the case of consumer debt not secured by the debtor's real property, the court must approve the agreement. This will be done only if the agreement will not impose undue hardship on the debtor; it must be in his/her best interests, and be made in good faith. It must be done to settle dischargeability or to provide for redemption of collateral.

Commonly Asked Questions About Bankruptcy

Q. Can husband and wife file joint bankruptcy?

A. Yes. This may be advisable if debts have been acquired jointly. Both spouses must agree to joint filing. A debtor cannot involve his/her spouse without the spouse's consent.

Q. *Need I be employed to declare bankruptcy?*

A. No, since any debt repayment is to come from liquidation of assets, not from income. Actually, unemployment is a major cause of bankruptcy.

Q. *Are my rights as a citizen affected?*

A. No. You may still vote, get licenses, own property, engage in business, receive unemployment compensation if out of work, etc. The new law greatly strengthens your rights in these regards.

Q. *What if I don't have the necessary cash to pay the fee?*

A. The fee can be paid in installments, by filing an additional form requesting this.

Q. *Where can I get help if I don't have funds for a lawyer?*

A. A lawyer may be agreeable to receiving his/her fee in installments, so a large amount of cash may not be necessary. It may be possible to hire a lawyer on an hourly basis. The expense will be reduced if you do much of the clerical work yourself and use the lawyer's time for answering legal questions, checking the forms, and appearing with you in court. If you are below federal poverty guidelines, you may be able to obtain assistance from the Legal Aid Society.

Q. *When is bankruptcy effective?*

A. As soon as the individual files for bankruptcy, he/she is temporarily relieved of payment of debts, so that, in this sense, it is effective immediately. Creditors are stayed from pressing their claims immediately. The situation becomes permanent when the court issues a discharge.

Q. *What do I do if a creditor keeps calling after I have petitioned for bankruptcy?*

A. A creditor cannot prevent you from filing for bankruptcy. After the forms are filed, the court should notify your creditors. If one does call you, tell him/her that you are bankrupt and give the case number. If you are harassed, you may be able to sue successfully. After bankruptcy, do not make any payment on a debt that has been discharged, as this could revive the debt. To avoid this possibility, one advisor suggests that no business be done with the former creditor.

Q. *What if a creditor with a non-dischargeable debt does not file a claim?*

A. It is to the advantage of the debtor or a guarantor of such debt to file the claim on behalf of the creditor.

Q. *What responsibilities do I have for my relatives' debts?*

A. For the most part, none. In the case of minor children, there would be little reason to go bankrupt since they are, for the most part, not legally liable for debts. In the case of a spouse, the situation is more complex. If the spouse has signed for your debts, as is common in purchasing major items, the responsibility is shared. Your responsibility for debts which your spouse may have run up depends on whether necessities or luxuries were purchased. There is generally no responsibility for other relatives.

Q. *Doesn't a bankruptcy ruin my credit record?*

A. A bankruptcy can remain on your credit record for up to ten years. Since you cannot declare bankruptcy more than once every six years, the creditor has considerable protection in extending new credit to you immediately following your bankruptcy. You should use the fresh start to develop a good credit record.

Filling Out the Forms

Most people have had some exposure to filling out government forms and might justifiably assume that completing a set of bankruptcy forms would be a complex task. While legal terms cannot be avoided in such documents, the forms are relatively straight-forward, and include clear-cut instructions for their completion. The forms have undergone relatively little change over the years. An individual inspecting the current bankruptcy forms would find little change in format or instructions from the forms used twenty or more years ago. Most of the alterations which have occurred have simplified the procedure. This is also likely to be true for new forms which have resulted from the new bankruptcy law.

Altogether, there are thirty official bankruptcy forms used in different situations. They are listed below:

OFFICIAL BANKRUPTCY FORMS

(Note — These official forms should be observed and used with such alterations as may be appropriate to suit the circumstances.)

Form	
No. 1.	Petition for Voluntary Bankruptcy
No. 2.	Application To Pay Filing Fees in Installments
No. 3.	Order Permitting Payment of Filing Fees in Installments
No. 4.	Verification on Behalf of a Corporation
No. 5.	Verification on Behalf of a Partnership
No. 6.	Schedules
No. 7.	Statement of Affairs for Bankrupt Not Engaged in Business

No. 8.	Statement of Affairs for Bankrupt Engaged in Business
No. 9.	Creditors' Petition for Bankruptcy
No. 10.	Summons to Bankrupt
No. 11.	Adjudication of Bankruptcy
No. 12.	Order for First Meeting of Creditors and Related Orders, Combined with Notice Thereof and of Automatic Stay
No. 13.	General Power of Attorney
No. 14.	Special Power of Attorney
No. 15.	Proof of Claim
No. 16.	Proof of Claim for Wages, Salary, or Commissions
No. 16A.	Proof of Multiple Claims for Wages, Salary, or Commissions
No. 17.	Order Approving Election of Trustee or Appointing Trustee and Fixing the Amount of his Bond
No. 18.	Notice to Trustee of his Election or Appointment and of Time for Filing a Complaint Objecting to Discharge of Bankrupt
No. 19.	Bond of Trustee or Receiver
No. 20.	Order Approving Trustee's Bond
No. 21.	Order That No Trustee Be Appointed
No. 22.	Report of Exempt Property
No. 23.	Order Approving Report of Exemptions
No. 24.	Discharge of Bankrupt
No. 25.	Caption for Adversary Proceeding
No. 26.	Summons and Notice of Trial of Adversary Proceeding
No. 27.	Subpoena to Witness
No. 28.	Notice of Appeal to a District Court from a Judgment or Order of a Referee Entered in Adversary Proceeding
No. 29.	Order and Notice for Final Meeting of Creditors
No. 30.	Report of Trustee in No-Asset Case

Fortunately, not all forms would have to be submitted in any given bankruptcy. Innovative publishers of legal forms have also reduced the number by combining similar forms, with only minor differences, into one. Consequently, the typical set of bankruptcy forms sold by legal stationery businesses might include the following:

1. Instruction sheet
2. Voluntary Petition
3. Schedules and others
4. Statement of Affairs

5. Statement of Compensation
6. Creditors list
7. Worksheets, heavy-duty envelopes, and covers

The forms come in sets of four, with the original and two copies to be filed, and the remaining form to be retained for your personal records. Worksheets are also included. The forms should be typed, but the court would accept them printed clearly in ink. Use of the worksheet form should minimize making errors on the final forms. When typographical errors occur, they can be marked out with x's. An honest error of fact would not be subject to severe criticism.

Filing the forms consists of delivering the forms to the court clerk, whose office is in the bankruptcy court serving your area. The person filing the forms does not have to personally deliver them. Someone else can deliver them, or they can be mailed to the court clerk. The filing fee is $50, but this can be paid in installments by filing an appropriate form.

Separate signatures are required on the Petition, the Statement of Affairs, the Oath, and the Schedules A and B. These signatures should be notarized. While the copies may be carbon or photocopies, the signatures and notarization should be original on each copy.

The first of the forms is the Petition for Voluntary Bankruptcy, a copy of which can be found on following page:

UNITED STATES BANKRUPTCY COURT FOR THE DISTRICT OF Case No.

*In re

Debtor — Include here all names used by debtor within last 6 years.

CHAPTER 7

VOLUNTARY CASE:
DEBTOR'S *JOINT* PETITION[1]

(If this form is used for joint petitioners wherever the word "petitioner" or words referring to petitioners are used they shall be read as if in the plural.)

1. Petitioner's post-office address is

2. Petitioner has
- ☐ resided within this district for the preceding 180 days.
- ☐ had his*(her)* domicile within this district for the preceding 180 days.
- ☐ had his*(her)* principal place of business within this district for the preceding 180 days.
- ☐ resided or been domiciled or had his*(her)* principal place of business within this district for a longer portion of the preceding 180 days than in any other district.

3. Petitioner is qualified to file this petition and is entitled to the benefits of title 11, United States Code as a voluntary debtor.

Wherefore, petitioner prays for relief in accordance with chapter 7 of title 11, United States Code.

Signed:...
Attorney for Petitioner

Address:...

....

Petitioner(s) signs if not represented by attorney

....
Petitioner

....
Petitioner

DECLARATION[2]

INDIVIDUAL: I, the petitioner named in the foregoing petition, certify under penalty of perjury that the foregoing is true and correct.

JOINT INDIVIDUALS: We. and the petitioners named in the foregoing petition. certify under penalty of perjury that the foregoing is true and correct.

CORPORATION: I, the of the corporation named as petitioner in the foregoing petition. certify under penalty of perjury that the foregoing is true and correct, and that the filing of this petition on behalf of the corporation has been authorized.

PARTNERSHIP: I. *a member — an authorized agent* — of the partnership named as petitioner in the foregoing petition. certify under penalty of perjury that the foregoing is true and correct. and that the filing of this petition on behalf of the partnership has been authorized.

Executed on 19 Signature:...
Petitioner

....
Petitioner

Form Nos. 1 & 2 combined & 5. chapter 7. Voluntary case: debtor's petition individual, joint, corporation and partnership. 10-79.

1 The filing of a joint petition is authorized by 11 U.S.C. §302.
2 The unsworn declaration conforms with Public Law 94-550, 90 Stat. 2534, 28 U.S.C. §1746 (1976) which permits the declaration to be made in the form indicated with the same force and effect as a sworn statement.
3069 Form Nos. 1, 2 & 5. chapter 7

To fill in the proper District number, refer to the Appendix. In the block beginning "In re," you should include all names used in the last six years. A woman who has married during this time period would include her maiden name after her married name. A business owner would include the name of the business or partnership. Social Security Number should also be included. You complete Item 2 by checking the appropriate box. This particular form is used as a joint petition, but also may be used for an individual. You should sign in the space noted "Petitioner" and have your signature notarized.

The second form is Schedule A, which has the following subsections:

Schedule A-1
Creditors having priority over other creditors.
Schedule A-2
Creditors holding security. This would include creditors holding mortgages, conditional sales contracts, or other collateral to secure their debt.
Schedule A-3
Creditors having unsecured claims without priority. This is the most important schedule, as it should include the bulk of the creditors and represent the greatest amount of debt.

Older forms also included a Schedule A-4, referring primarily to checks made payable to the debtor which were transferred to a creditor but returned unpaid. Another such older form is a Schedule A-5, which refers to co-signed debts. These claims are not segregated on the new forms, but are to be included in Schedule A-1, A-2, or A-3. This depends on whether they are priority claims, secured, or unsecured, respectively. Schedule A-1, which lists creditors having priority claims, can be found on the following page.

UNITED STATES BANKRUPTCY COURT FOR THE ______ DISTRICT OF ______

Case No.

In re

Debtor ______ Include here all named used by debtor within last 6 years.

Schedule A — STATEMENT OF ALL LIABILITIES OF DEBTOR

(If this form is used by joint debtors wherever the word "debtor" or words referring to debtor are used they shall be read as if in the plural.)

Schedules A-1, A-2, and A-3 must include all the claims against the debtor(s) or debtors' property as of the date of the filing of the petition by or against debtor.

SCHEDULE A-1 — CREDITORS HAVING PRIORITY

(1) Nature of Claim	(2) Name of creditor and complete mailing address including zip code (if unknown, so state)	(3) Specify when claim was incurred and the consideration therefor; when claim is contingent, unliquidated, disputed, or subject to setoff, evidenced by a judgment, negotiable instrument, or other writing, or incurred as partner or joint contractor, so indicate; specify name of any partner or joint contractor on any debt.	(4) Indicate if claim is contingent, unliquidated or disputed.	(5) Amount of Claim
a. Wages, salary, and commissions, including vacation, severance and sick leave pay owing to workmen, servants, clerks, or traveling or city salesmen on salary or commission basis, whole or part time, whether or not selling exclusively for the debtor, not exceeding $2,000 to each, earned within 90 days before filing of petition or cessation of business, if earlier (specify date).				$
b. Contributions to employee benefit plans for services rendered within 180 days before filing of petition or cessation of business, if earlier (specify date).				
c. Deposits by individuals, not exceeding $900 for each for purchase, lease, or rental of property or services for personal, family, or household use that were not delivered or provided				
d. Taxes owing (itemize by type of tax and taxing authority.) (1) To the United States (2) To any State (3) To any other taxing authority				
			Total	

Form No. 6, Schedule A-1, 10-79

3072 Form No. 6, page 1

Annex rider if additional space necessary.

© 1979 JULIUS BLUMBERG, INC

This form asks that the debtor "specify when claim was incurred." If an exact date is not known, an approximate date should be indicated. Some explanation might be helpful of several legal terms used in this form.

Across the top, the form asks when a claim was incurred and what "consideration" was received. One of the requirements of contracts is that a promise will be enforced only when it has been paid for or purchased. In filling out this form, you would list the item of merchandise or services you received in return for incurring the debt.

A second term, "contingent," refers to a debt which exists but is indefinite in amount. The law does not know how much the claim is worth and permits the parties to bargain over the amount. The term "disputed" applies if there is a disagreement as to whether any money at all is owed.

"Subject to setoff" is a term which is most applicable in the case of bank accounts. If you have a checking account balance with the same bank at which you have a loan, the bank may put a hold on the funds in the checking account to protect its outstanding loan. The individual who had planned ahead would have used funds from the checking account in such an instance for consumption or investment in exempt assets.

This form also asks whether the debt is evidenced by a judgement, negotiable instrument, or other writing. A "judgement" is a court decision ruling on the obligations of the parties to a lawsuit. A "negotiable instrument" is a security, such as a note, which may be transferred by endorsing it to a third party.

Schedule A-1 covers priority creditors, which are primarily:

1. Employees to whom you owe wages, not in excess of $2,000 each, earned within three months of filing the petition.
2. The United States or any state or municipality to whom taxes are owed.
3. Other creditors have priority by law.

Schedule A-2 covers Creditors Holding Security. In addition to the information requested in Schedule A-1, this schedule asks for a description of the security interest, chattel mortgage, conditional sales contract, or collateral security for any debt. Secured loans are usually those for appliances, cars, furniture and household goods, home improvement loans, and chattel mortgages covering loans made against personal property.

Schedule A-3 covers unsecured debts, which would usually include utility bills, credit card purchases, department store credit, medical bills, personal loans, and food bills. In effect, any bill not included in Schedules A-1 and A-2 would be listed in Schedule A-3. An apartment lease should be included, giving the total amount due for the remainder of the lease, designated as "unliquidated." This is because the amount due will depend on whether the apartment can be sublet and, if so, at what rate.

Schedules A-2 and A-3 have been combined on one page by the publishers of this set of forms, and appear on the following page. In the kit you can order from them are two extra full-page Schedule A-3 forms.

Schedule A-2 — Creditors Holding Security

(1) Name of creditor and complete mailing address including zip code (if unknown, so state)	(2) Description of security and date when obtained by creditor	(3) Specify when claim was incurred and the consideration therefor; when claim is contingent, unliquidated, disputed, subject to setoff, evidenced by a judgment, negotiable instrument, or other writing, or incurred as partner or joint contractor, so indicate; specify name of any partner or joint contractor on any debt.	(4) Indicate if claim is contingent, unliquidated or disputed	(5) Market value	(6) Amount of claim without deduction of value of security
				$	$
			Total		

Schedule A-3 — Creditors Having Unsecured Claims Without Priority

Name of creditor (including last known holder of any negotiable instrument) complete mailing address including zip code (if unknown, so state).	Specify when claim was incurred and the consideration therefor; when claim is contingent, unliquidated, disputed, subject to setoff, evidenced by a judgment, negotiable instrument, or other writing, or incurred as partner or joint contractor, so indicate; specify name of any partner or joint contractor on any debt.	Amount of Claim
		$
	Total	

Form No 6. Schedule A-2 & A-3. 10-79

3072 Form Nos 6. page 2

Annex rider if additional space necessary.

© 1979 JULIUS BLUMBERG INC

Schedule B is a list of all assets and is divided into four subschedules:

Schedule B-1 . . . . . Real Property
Schedule B-2 . . . . . Personal Property
Schedule B-3 . . . . . Property not otherwise scheduled
Schedule B-4 . . . . Exempt Property.

Schedule B-1, covering real estate, has been revised in recent years to reflect gross value of real estate rather than net value. The mortgage of a property would be listed in Schedule A-2, and is not deducted from market value in Schedule B-1. The value of real estate should be contained by having the property appraised by a Realtor, not by using original purchase price.

Schedule B-2 covers holdings of personal property which, for all practical purposes, include all property which is not classified as real estate. Even if property is claimed as exempt, it must still be listed in Schedule B-2, as well as in Schedule B-4. **Schedule B-2** lists property in twenty-two different categories, but the average individual can answer "none" to most of these groups. A number of the groups pertain only to business owners or farmers.

Schedule B-1 and B-2 have been combined on one page, with **B-2** being continued on a second page. These schedules are reproduced on the following pages.

SCHEDULE B — STATEMENT OF ALL PROPERTY OF DEBTOR

Schedules B-1, B-2, B-3, and B-4 must include all property of the debtor as of the date of the filing of the petition by or against debtor.

Schedule B-1 — Real Property

Description and location of all real property in which debtor has an interest (including equitable and future interests, interests in estates by the entirety, community property, life estates, leaseholds, and rights and powers exercisable for the benefit of debtor)	Nature of interest (specify all deeds and written instruments relating thereto)	Market value of debtor's interest without deduction for secured claims listed in schedule A-2 or exemptions claimed in schedule B-4	
		$	
	Total		

Schedule B-2 — Personal Property

Type of Property	Description and location	Market value of debtor's interest without deduction for secured claims listed on schedule A-2 or exemptions claimed in schedule B-4	
a. Cash on hand		$	
b. Deposits of money with banking institutions, savings and loan associations, credit unions, public utility companies, landlords, and others			
c. Household goods, supplies, and furnishings			
d. Books, pictures, and other art objects; stamp, coin, and other collections			
e. Wearing apparel, jewelry, firearms, sports equipment, and other personal possessions			
f. Automobiles, trucks, trailers, and other vehicles			
g. Boats, motors, and their accessories			
	Total		

Form No. 6. Schedule B-1 & B-2. 10-79

3072 Form No. 6. page 5

Annex rider if additional space necessary.

© 1979 JULIUS BLUMBERG, INC

Schedule B-2 — Personal Property (Continued)

Type of property	Description and location	Market value of debtor's interest without deduction for secured claims listed on schedule A-2 or exemptions claimed in schedule B-4	
h. Livestock, poultry, and other animals		$	
i. Farming supplies and implements			
j. Office equipment, furnishings, and supplies			
k. Machinery, fixtures, equipment, and supplies (other than those listed in items j and l) used in business			
l. Inventory			
m. Tangible personal property of any other description			
n. Patents, copyrights, franchises, and other general intangibles (specify all documents and writings relating thereto)			
o. Government and corporate bonds and other negotiable and nonnegotiable instruments			
p. Other liquidated debts owing debtor			
q. Contingent and unliquidated claims of every nature, including counterclaims of the debtor (give estimated value of each)			
r. Interests in insurance policies (itemize surrender or refund values of each)			
s. Annuities			
t. Stocks and interests in incorporated and unincorporated companies (itemize separately)			
u. Interests in partnerships			
v. Equitable and future interests, life estates, and rights or powers exercisable for the benefit of the debtor (other than those listed in schedule B-1) [specify all written instruments relating thereto]	Total		

Form No. 6. Schedule B-2 (Continued). 10-79

3072 Form No. 6, page 6

Schedule B-3 covers property not otherwise scheduled. Primarily, this covers property transfers to creditors within the last four months, which subjects the transfers to particular scrutiny from the court. One of the major functions of the bankruptcy proceeding is to review recent transactions between debtor and creditor, to determine if one creditor is getting preferential treatment over other creditors in the same class.

Schedule B-4 is to include Property Claimed as Exempt. If the debtor has planned ahead, most assets should not exceed the exempt value for those items permitted by the state residence. A summary of state exemptions is covered in the Appendix. A list of federal exemptions is included in the previous chapter.

Reproductions of Schedules B-3 and B-4 are found below and on the following page.

Schedule B-3 — Property Not Otherwise Scheduled

Type of property	Description and location	Market value of debtor's interest without deduction for secured claims listed in schedule A-2 or exemptions claimed in schedule B-4	
a. Property transferred under assignment for benefit of creditors, within 120 days prior to filing of petition (specify date of assignment, name and address of assignee, amount realized therefrom by the assignee, and disposition of proceeds so far as known to debtor)		$	
b. Property of any kind not otherwise scheduled			
	Total		

Debtor selects the following property as exempt pursuant to ☐ 11 U.S.C. §522(d) ☐ the laws of the State of ....

Schedule B-4 — Property Claimed as Exempt

Type of property	Location, description, and so far as relevant to the claim of exemption, present use of property	Specify statute creating the exemption	Value claimed exempt
			$
		Total	

Form No 6. Schedule B-3 & B-4. 10-79

3072 Form No. 6. page 7

Annex rider if additional space necessary.

© 1979 JULIUS BLUMBERG. INC

A summary of debts and property then follows, based on the preceding schedules.

Finally, an oath to Schedules A and B completes this form. The section beginning with "Individual" is completed, and the form is signed and notarized.

A reproduction of this form appears on the following page.

SUMMARY OF DEBTS AND PROPERTY (From the statements of the debtor in Schedule A and B)

Schedule		Total
	DEBTS	
A 1 a, b	Wages, etc. having priority	
A 1(c)	Deposits of money	
A 1 (d)1	Taxes owing United States	
A-1 (d)2	Taxes owing states	
A-1 (d)3	Taxes owing other taxing authorities	
A-2	Secured claims	
A-3	Unsecured claims without priority	
	Schedule A total	
	PROPERTY	
B-1	Real property (total value)	
B-2 a	Cash on hand	
B 2 b	Deposits	
B-2 c	Household goods	
B-2 d	Books, pictures, and collections	
B-2 e	Wearing apparel and personal possessions	
B 2 f	Automobiles and other vehicles	
B-2 g	Boats, motors, and accessories	
B-2 h	Livestock and other animals	
B 2 i	Farming supplies and implements	
B 2 j	Office equipment and supplies	
B-2 k	Machinery, equipment, and supplies used in business	
B 2 l	Inventory	
B 2 m	Other tangible personal property	
B 2 n	Patents and other general intangibles	
B 2 o	Bonds and other instruments	
B-2 p	Other liquidated debts	
B-2 q	Contingent and unliquidated claims	
B 2 r	Interests in insurance policies	
B-2 s	Annuities	
B 2 t	Interests in corporations and unincorporated companies	
B-2 u	Interests in partnerships	
B 2 v	Equitable and future interests, rights, and powers in personalty	
B-3 a	Property assigned for benefit of creditors	
B-3 b	Property not otherwise scheduled	
	Schedule B total	

UNSWORN DECLARATION UNDER PENALTY OF PERJURY

INDIVIDUAL(S): I(*we*) *and* certify under penalty of perjury that I(*we*) have read the foregoing schedules, consisting of sheets, and that they are true and correct to the best of my(*our*) knowledge, information, and belief.

CORPORATION: I, the (*insert president or other officer or an authorized agent*) of the corporation named as debtor in this case, certify under penalty of perjury that I have read the foregoing schedules, consisting of sheets, and that they are true and correct to the best of my knowledge, information, and belief.

PARTNERSHIP: I, a (*insert member or an authorized agent*) of the partnership named as debtor in this case, certify under penalty of perjury that I have read the foregoing schedules, consisting of sheets, and that they are true and correct to the best of my knowledge, information, and belief.

Executed on 19 Signature Signature

Form 6 Summary of debts & property declarations

© 1979 JULIUS BLUMBERG, INC

3072 Form No. 6, page 8

The second major form is the "Statement of Affairs," which has comprehensive instructions for completion. The name must coincide with that on the Petition. A number of questions are intended to eliminate the possibility of fraudulent transfers of property or preferential treatment of any one creditor. In the case of any loan repaid in the last twelve months, the debtor must be able to prove that the loan was made in good faith and for fair consideration. The Statement of Affairs must be signed and notarized. A reproduction of this form appears on the following pages.

UNITED STATES BANKRUPTCY COURT FOR THE DISTRICT OF

Case No.

In re

Debtor

Include here all names used by debtor within last 6 years.

STATEMENT OF FINANCIAL AFFAIRS FOR DEBTOR NOT ENGAGED IN BUSINESS

Each question should be answered or the failure to answer explained. If the answer is "none," this should be stated. If additional space is needed for the answer to any question, a separate sheet, properly identified, and made a part hereof, should be used and attached.

The term "original petition," as used in the following questions, shall mean the petition filed under Rule 1002, 1003, or 1004.

(If this form is used by joint debtors wherever the word "debtor" or words referring to debtor are used they shall be read as if in the plural.)

1. Name and residence.

a. What is your full name and social security number?

b. Have you used, or been known by, any other names within the 6 years immediately preceding the filing of the original petition herein?
(If so, give particulars.)

c. Where do you now reside?

d. Where else have you resided during the 6 years immediately preceding the filing of the original petition herein?

2. Occupation and income.

a. What is your occupation?

b. Where are you now employed?
(Give the name and address of your employer, or the address at which you carry on your trade or profession, and the length of time you have been so employed or engaged.)

c. Have you been in a partnership with anyone, or engaged in any business during the 6 years immediately preceding the filing of the original petition herein?
(If so, give particulars, including names, dates, and places.)

d. What amount of income have you received from your trade or profession during each of the 2 calendar years immediately preceding the filing of the original petition herein?

e. What amount of income have you received from other sources during each of these 2 years?
(Give particulars, including each source, and the amount received therefrom.)

3. Tax returns and refunds.

a. Where did you file your federal and state income tax returns for the 2 years immediately preceding the filing of the original petition herein?

b. What tax refunds (income and other) have you received during the year immediately preceding the filing of the original petition herein?

c. To what tax refunds (income or other), if any, are you, or may you be, entitled?
(Give particulars, including information as to any refund payable jointly to you and your spouse or any other person.)

4. Bank accounts and safe deposit boxes.

a. What bank accounts have you maintained alone or together with any other person, and in your own or any other name within the 2 years immediately preceding the filing of the original petition herein?
(Give the name and address of each bank, the name in which the deposit is maintained, and the name and address of every other person authorized to make withdrawals from such account.)

b. What safe deposit box or boxes or other depository or depositories have you kept or used for your securities, cash, or other valuables within the 2 years immediately preceding the filing of the original petition herein?
(Give the name and address of the bank or other depository, the name in which each box or other depository was kept, the name and address of every other person who had the right of access thereto, a brief description of the contents thereof, and, if the box has been surrendered, state when surrendered, or, if transferred, when transferred, and the name and address of the transferee.)

5. Books and records.

a. Have you kept books of account or records relating to your affairs within the 2 years immediately preceding the filing of the original petition herein?

b. In whose possession are these books or records?
(Give names and addresses.)

c. If any of these books or records are not available, explain.

d. Have any books of account or records relating to your affairs been destroyed, lost or otherwise disposed of within the 2 years immediately preceding the filing of the original petition herein?
(If so, give particulars, including date of destruction, loss, or disposition, and reason therefor.)

6. Property held for another person.

What property do you hold for any other person?
(Give name and address of each person, and describe the property, or value thereof, and all writings relating thereto.)

7. Prior bankruptcy.

What proceedings under the Bankruptcy Act or title 11, United States Code have previously been brought by or against you?
(State the location of the bankruptcy court, the nature and number of each case, the date when it was filed, and whether a discharge was granted or refused, the case was dismissed, or a composition, arrangement, or plan was confirmed.)

Form No. 7. statement of affairs: not engaged in business: page 1. 10-79

3076 Form No. 7. page 1

Annex rider if additional space necessary.

8. Receiverships, general assignments, and other modes of liquidation.

a. Was any of your property, at the time of the filing of the original petition herein, in the hands of a receiver, trustee, or other liquidating agent? (If so, give a brief description of the property, the name and address of the receiver, trustee, or other agent, and, if the agent was appointed in a court proceeding, the name and location of the court the title and number of the case, and the nature of the proceeding.)

b. Have you made any assignment of your property for the benefit of your creditors, or any general settlement with your creditors, within one year immediately preceding the filing of the original petition herein?
(If so, give dates, the name and address of the assignee, and a brief statement of the terms of assignment or settlement.)

9. Property in hands of third person.

Is any other person holding anything of value in which you have an interest? (Give name and address, location and description of the property, and circumstances of the holding.)

10. Suits, executions, and attachments.

a. Were you a party to any suit pending at the time of the filing of the original petition herein? (If so, give the name and location of the court and the title and nature of the proceeding.)

b. Were you a party to any suit terminated within the year immediately preceding the filing of the original petition herein.? (If so, give the name and location of the court, the title and nature of the proceeding, and the result.)

c. Has any of your property been attached, garnished, or seized under any legal or equitable process within the year immediately preceding the filing of the original petition herein? (If so, describe the property seized or person garnished, and at whose suit.)

11. Loans repaid.

What repayments on loans in whole or in part have you made during the year immediately preceding the filing of the original petition herein?
(Give the name and address of the lender, the amount of the loan and when received, the amounts and dates of payments and, if the lender is a relative or insider, the relationship.)

12. Transfers of property.

a. Have you made any gifts, other than ordinary and usual presents to family members and charitable donations, during the year immediately preceding the filing of the original petition herein? (If so, give names and addresses of donees and dates, description, and value of gifts.)

b. Have you made any other transfer, absolute or for the purpose of security, or any other disposition, of real or tangible personal property during the year immediately preceding the filing of the original petition herein? (Give a description of the property, the date of the transfer or disposition, to whom transferred or how disposed of, and, if the transferee is a relative or insider, the relationship, the consideration, if any, received therefor, and the disposition of such consideration.)

13. Repossessions and returns.

Has any property been returned to, or repossessed by, the seller or by a secured party during the year immediately preceding the filing of the original petition herein?
(If so, give particulars including the name and address of the party getting the property and its description and value.)

14. Losses.

a. Have you suffered any losses from fire, theft, or gambling during the year immediately preceding or since the filing of the original petition herein? (If so, give particulars, including dates, names, and places, and the amounts of money or value and general description of property lost.)

b. Was the loss covered in whole or part by insurance?
(If so, give particulars.)

15. Payments or transfers to attorneys.

a. Have you consulted an attorney during the year immediately preceding or since the filing of the original petition herein? (Give date, name, and address.)

b. Have you during the year immediately preceding or since the filing of the original petition herein paid any money or transferred any property to the attorney or to any other person on his behalf?
(If so, give particulars, including amount paid or value of property transferred and date of payment or transfer.)

c. Have you, either during the year immediately preceding or since the filing of the original petition herein, agreed to pay any money or transfer any property to an attorney at law, or to any other person on his behalf?
(If so, give particulars, including amount and terms of obligation.)

UNSWORN DECLARATION UNDER PENALTY OF PERJURY

I *(We)*, *and*

certify under penalty of perjury that I *(we)* have read the foregoing schedules, consisting of sheets, and that they are true and correct to the best of my *(our)* knowledge, information, and belief.

Executed on 19

Signature Signature

Form No. 7, statement of affairs: not engaged in business: page 2, 10-79

3076 Form No. 7, page 2 Annex rider if additional space necessary.

© 1979 JULIUS BLUMBERG INC

Bankruptcy or Reorganization for the Business Owner

The problem of bankruptcy or reorganization for a giant, complex business is obviously beyond the scope of this book. However, for the small business, the process of bankruptcy or reorganization may be little different than personal bankruptcy.

For example, Chapter 13 has been broadened to include individuals with stable income; whereas, it had been restricted to wage earners previously. As a result, individual debtors engaged in business can now seek relief under Chapter 13, provided that unsecured debts are less than $100,000 and secured debts are less than $350,000. For other businesses seeking reorganization, Chapter 11 of the bankruptcy code has been broadened and improved to help businesses seeking a new start.

In this chapter, the following areas will be covered:

1. Some differences in procedures and forms for the business owner declaring bankruptcy.
2. Scope and magnitude of business bankruptcies today.
3. The danger of accelerating bankruptcies in the years ahead, and how the business owner can minimize personal exposure.

Differences in Forms and Procedures

Much of the difference between personal and business bankruptcy is due to the larger size of the average business bankruptcy. This makes it more time-consuming, complex, and expensive.

In the Brookings study on bankruptcy mentioned earlier, the average time for a business bankruptcy case was found to be twenty-three months. This is almost twice that of a personal bankruptcy case. In business cases, priority creditors received 26% of the amounts proved and allowed; whereas, in personal bankruptcies, the comparable figure was only 13%. In business cases, secured creditors received 31% of amounts proved and allowed; whereas, the figure for personal bankruptcies averaged only 8%.

In both personal and business bankruptcies, the unsecured creditors averaged less than 10% of the amounts proved and allowed. The amounts would have been an even lower percentage, except that many creditors did not even bother to prove their claims. The median scheduled assets in business cases were $12,000, but only about $3,000 of this was collected. In contrast, median debts were $40,000.

A second major difference between business and personal bankruptcy arises when the business is incorporated. In my book, **How To Form Your Own Corporation Without A Lawyer For Under $50,** I discuss the advantages and disadvantages of incorporating. As pointed out there, one of the corporation's major advantages is that the personal liability of the owner is limited to the amount of money put into the corporation, with the exception of unpaid taxes. In contrast, in a proprietorship or partnership, the owners are personally liable for all debts and judgements against the business, including liability in case of failure or other disaster. In a partnership, each member can bind the other so that one partner can cause the other to be personally liable. Because a corporation by definition has limited liability, it is not important that a corporation receive a discharge from debts unless it intends to stay in business. In contrast, discharge from debt is the crucial objective in declaring personal bankruptcy.

Technically, those corporations attempting to stay in business under the protection of our bankruptcy laws are not asking to be declared bankrupt. They are petitioning for reorganization.

Businesses petitioning for liquidation or straight bankruptcy do so under Chapter 7 of the code. With the exception of individual people eligible to file under Chapter 13, businesses seeking to reorganize do so under Chapter 11.

Chapter 11 is similar in many respects to Chapter 13, as it provides a plan for settlement or extension of time for payment of debts. Chapter 11 is applicable to individual partnerships and corporations with the exception of insurance companies and certain financial institutions. Also excluded are stock brokers and commodity brokers.

A Chapter 11 plan shall:

1. Designate classes of claims, specifying those which are not impaired under the plan.
2. Specify any classes of claims which are impaired and how they are to be treated.
3. Provide same treatment for each class of claim, unless holder of a particular claim agrees to less favorable treatment.
4. Provide adequate means for the plan's execution, such as:
    a. Retention by debtor of all or any part of the property held.
    b. Transfer any or all property to other entities.
    c. Merger with others.
    d. Sale of any part of the property or distribution of property among those having an interest.
    e. Satisfaction or modification of any liens.
    f. Curing or waiving any default.
    g. Capital changes, such as modification of debt obligations or issuance of other securities.
5. Provision for assumption or rejection of executory contracts or unexpired leases of debtor.

While much of the publicity about business bankruptcies refers to Chapter 11 cases, most small businesses file for straight bankruptcy. In the Brookings study, this was true of 90% of the small businesses.

The straight bankruptcy procedure is the same for business as it is for personal bankruptcy, starting with the Petition. Creditors are more likely to show up for the "first meeting of creditors," but they tend to be inactive. The Brookings study pointed out that restraining orders were almost never needed in personal bankruptcy cases. In 24% of the business cases, they were requested to prevent creditors from trying to collect before the proceeding was finished.

A partnership is considered a separate legal entity in bankruptcy proceedings, separate and distinct from its members. It may be adjudged a bankrupt without the individual partners being so adjudged, or it may be adjudged bankrupt along with one or more of the general partners.

If a petition is filed on behalf of a partnership by fewer than all of the general partners, it must allege that the partnership is insolvent. The partnership property must first be applied to their individual debts. Any surplus of any partner is applied to the partnership debts, after paying individual debts, and vice versa. In the event that one or more, but not all, of the partners are adjudged bankrupts, the partnership property cannot be administered in bankruptcy except with the consent of the general partners not adjudged bankrupt. However, the latter must settle the partnership business as quickly as possible.

In the case of corporations, the directors of a corporation have the power to file a petition in voluntary bankruptcy. In some states, however, they may require authorization of stockholders. An officer of the corporation would have to be given this authority by the directors in order to file a bankruptcy petition.

The Statement of Affairs for businesses includes much the same as is included for bankrupts not engaged in business, but requests the additional following information:

1. Nature and location of business.
2. Financial statements.
3. Inventories.
4. Income other than from operations of business.
5. Accounts and other receivables.
6. Business leases.
7. Withdrawals.
8. Members of partnership: officers, directors, managers, and principal stockholders of the corporation.

A complete Statement of Affairs for bankrupts, including comprehensive instructions for completing the forms for those engaged in business, is included in the Appendix.

Scope and Magnitude of Business Bankruptcies Today

The rate of business failure has always been high, even in favorable economic times. This is not apparent from bankruptcy figures, since many companies go out of business by selling out to others, filing for reorganization, or simply closing down.

The economy in the last decade has been far from favorable, as inflationary pressure has become uncontrollable. Our economy has suffered from an inflationary bias since the 1930's, but high rates of inflation have been concentrated in or after periods of war. The burst of inflation in the first half of the 1970's was attributed to President Johnson's "guns and butter" decisions, which superimposed expenditures for the "Great Society" programs upon the already high level of government expenditures for the Vietnam War. However, inflation has continued long past the end of the last war, indicating how permanently it is imbedded in the fabric of our economy and society.

The federal government has not been the only governmental body to contribute to inflation. State and local government expenditures were less than 6% of our Gross National Product in 1947, but increased to 8% in 1957, 11% in 1967, and 14% in the 1970's. Total government spending has increased from 9% of national income to 40% in the last forty years. Government also contributed directly to reported inflation by imposition of various so-called consumer protection and pollution-control legislation. These diverted substantial amounts of capital expenditures by the private sector of the economy into non-productive uses.

The government's response to inflationary pressures has been to try by various measures, including price controls, to control the symptoms, not the causes.

Regulated Industries

The industries hurt first were those most under government controls. The regulated industries, such as electric utilities, were unable to raise prices nearly as fast as costs rose. While regulators were reluctant to permit the necessary price increases to finance the growth of the industry, they did encourage less conservative accounting, making earnings look larger. This did not produce additional *cash*, however, and the utilities had to increase borrowing. Eventually, the safety of their bonds and stocks deteriorated, so that this vital industry was threatened with stagnation.

The Defense Industry

The defense industry has been another victim of the economy. Many, if not most, of the defense companies had contracts with only limited protection against inflation. In the case of new technological products, it was extremely difficult to forecast the cost, particularly when contracts were subject to frequent modifications by the military. As costs skyrocketed, largely due to unexpectedly high rates of inflation, defense companies incurred substantial losses. Highly vocal opponents of the war were extremely critical of any aid to the defense companies, and many could have gone bankrupt if these critics had prevailed. Lockheed, which was rescued only by special government action, is the most famous near-victim. However, the problem was very widespread and numerous smaller companies, particularly in the military electronics field, disappeared.

Some industries were able to raise prices, but this was no guarantee of survival in an inflationary economy. One of the most controlled areas of inflation was the real estate industry, where cost and prices rose much faster than the economy. During the early 1970's, billions of dollars (much of it speculative) flowed into Real Estate Investment Trusts, which were created to finance the building industry. Unfortunately, the demand for most products diminishes as the price rises rapidly, so that the industry became overbuilt and unprofitable. Many leaders in the industry are near bankruptcy, kept alive by the banks which have made substantial loans to them and deign to see those loans become worthless. One of the largest companies in the industry recently reported that non-earning assets and foreclosed properties had increased to $448 million, or 94% of the total loans and investments!

Eventually, the spreading economic chaos hit the consumer directly, partly by increasing unemployment, and partly by reducing real income. Those industries unable to earn a satisfactory rate of return were unable to expand, so that shortages became widespread. The frustrated consumer found the basic necessities of life going up faster than income. As food shortages raised food prices, cost of gasoline and utilities rose, and dwelling costs soared. Consumer-oriented companies found themselves in financial trouble, along with the rest of the economy.

W. T. Grant Co., one of the country's largest retail chains, filed for protection under the Bankruptcy Act. Chrysler Corporation skirted on the edge of bankruptcy during the 1970's, and was rescued by government-guaranteed loans in 1980.

The Domino Effect

In looking at these individual bankruptcies, we must remember that they represent only the tip of the iceberg. A company the size of W. T. Grant has many suppliers who will feel the impact of its bankruptcy. Similarly, a bankruptcy by New York City would spread financial troubles broadly across the nation. To use an isolated example, the common stock of Pullman incurred substantial weakness in the stock market at the time New York's financial position deteriorated. One explanation for the weakness was that Pullman had a $200 million contract to deliver 750 mass transit cars to New York. One analyst felt the company would lose *only* $50 million, or about one-sixth of its book value, but would survive. But most companies, especially smaller ones, are not as strong financially as Pullman.

Financial problems are so widespread that the banking structure of the country has been undermined. In the following table, we can see the strain in 1975 on New York City banks caused by W. T. Grant, New York City, and the R.E.I.T. industry. Add to this the problem in consumer loans, where the delinquency rate was running at high levels. Also, defaults by large debtors tend to have a domino effect by triggering defaults throughout the economy.

**New York City Banks
Exposure to Major Debtor
Defaults**

Company	Total Equity 6/30/75	Estimated N.Y.C. Exposure[1]	W.T. Grant Exposure	Estimated R.E.I.T. Exposure[1]
	(millions)	(millions)	(millions)	(millions)
Chase Manhattan	$1,547	300	97	750
Citicorp	2,217	250	97	780
Chemical	761	275	40	720

Company	Total Equity 6/30/75	Estimated N.Y.C. Exposure[1]	W.T. Grant Exposure	Estimated R.E.I.T. Exposure[1]
	(millions)	(millions)	(millions)	(millions)
J. P. Morgan	1,104	225	97	295
Manufacturers	925	225	48	415
Bankers Trust	597	120	32	650

Following the financial crisis of 1974/75, a more conservative attitude developed among business managers, consumers, and government officials. Capital expenditures were restrained, inventories maintained at reasonable levels, and the economy expanded at a steady but gradual pace. In spite of the balanced growth in the economy, inflation was back to record levels by the end of the 1970's. Interest rates were also back to all-time highs, and appeared likely to remain high in spite of an economic slowdown.

How Business Owners Can Minimize Exposure to Risk of Bankruptcy

Today, the smart business owners are no longer concentrating on survival. When more speculative competitors have collapsed, survivors will be able to grow by picking up their share of the market.

Survival starts with a strong balance sheet. The credit of a customer is being scrutinized very carefully. The story is told of a salesman who had had a bad day being turned down by customer after customer. Finally, he was pleasantly amazed to be warmly greeted by a customer who bought everything he had to sell. His delight vanished a few days after the goods were shipped,

[1] Estimated exposure is taken from report, "The Banking Environment: Certain Concerns," by Goldman Sachs, November 10, 1975.

as the customer had declared bankruptcy. One is reminded of the advice: "If something sounds too good to be true, then it probably isn't."

Inventories are being reduced, permitting a reduction of borrowed money used to finance those inventories. In the inventory control field, a rule of thumb is that it costs 25¢ per annum, including interest, storage cost, and losses through theft and deterioration, to carry a dollar of inventory. With this much of a handicap, it is easier to lose money than make it by speculating in inventory.

As accounts receivable and inventory are reduced, a company can improve its financial position by either increasing cash or reducing debts with the money formerly tied up in the above areas. Business owners are also analyzing fixed assets carefully, which produce unsatisfactory or no profit, and are turning these assets into cash.

While the balance sheet is receiving renewed attention, the income statement is not being overlooked. Inflation forces the business owner to become more sophisticated in analyzing the income statement. Owners have become aware that standard accounting produces mythical profits during inflation. They may buy a product for $10 and then sell it for $20, but is there any profit if the same article costs them $20 when they replenish their inventories? They may not even have sufficient cash to buy the same article at the new price, since "big government" and "big labor" would demand a share in the profit, even though it is more imaginary than real. Similarly, depreciation charges against an older machine will be insufficient in providing funds to replace that machine during inflationary periods. Much of the profit reported by our heavy industries would disappear if the costs of depreciation were reported realistically to reflect inflation.

Attempts have been made by financial analysts to adjust corporate earnings for these distortions. Reported earnings in 1974 were almost triple earnings adjusted to remove the inflationary effect. Manufacturing corporations are earning only 4% on invested capital after the inflation adjustment, as compared to a 12% reported rate of return.

Since that time, the rate of return on invested capital has risen to over 16%. But the rate of inflation has also risen to keep the real rate of return at low levels.

When business fails to earn an adequate return on investment, it can temporarily meet part of its financial needs by drawing down its current assets or increasing its current liabilities. Business has been doing this at a rapid rate. Once excess cash is used up, corporations can also reduce accounts receivable by tightening up credit, or can borrow more heavily themselves from the banks or trade sources of credit. This process has already gone a long way, as illustrated by the chart which measures the Current Ratio, or ratio of current assets to current liabilities.

CURRENT RATIO OF MANUFACTURING CORPORATIONS

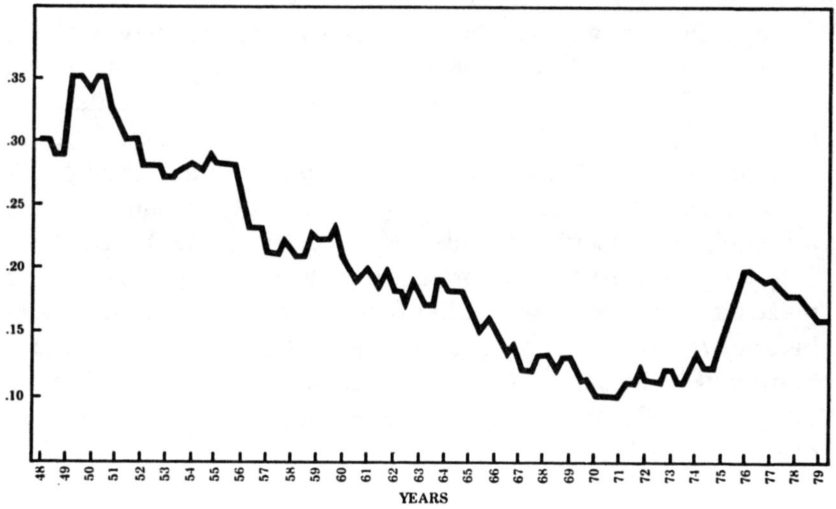

The chart offers some valuable insight into the reason that inflation and financial problems are closely linked. The business owner may feel very successful in early stages of inflation, as reported earnings look good. The owners want to expand, of course, in order to keep up with demand. Unfortunately, their real earnings are much less than reported earnings, so that they have to borrow money to finance their expansion.

At some point in the economic cycle, the government or Federal Reserve gets disturbed by the rising rate of inflation, and attempts to put on the brakes. At this point, the business owner can suddenly become very uncomfortable. Customers slow down their spending rate at a time when the owner's costs are reaching peak levels. The owner's situation is further aggravated by high interest expenses and high depreciation charges from high-cost plant or store space that has been recently added. The owner becomes a bankruptcy candidate.

The Good News

For the knowledgeable business owner, the period ahead can be one of opportunity, as less-able competitors fail to adjust to the difficult conditions. Large corporations discontinue low-profit margin business. The small business may be able to move into that area, and, with its lower overhead, make a good profit on it. In such cases, small business owners may be able to obtain the equipment to run the business far below cost. To be able to take advantage of the opportunities ahead, however, the owner must be able to stay on his/her feet, or, if knocked down, must be able to get back up again quickly. It is my hope that this book will be of help in this regard, through its advice on how to stay out of financial trouble, or how to get out — if you're in over your head.

A Final Note

How Americans Are Adapting to the Inflation/Recession Economy

The inflation/recession economy which has accelerated in intensity in recent years is in the process of producing widespread changes in American society. One long-term trend has been a substantial decline in the size of the American family. While this decline has been attributed to a number of factors, including highly-publicized dangers of over-population, a simple explanation may be that children are expensive. With smaller families, people can live comfortably in smaller houses, drive smaller cars, spend less on education, etc. In the case of younger families, couples are generally postponing children until the heavy expenses of starting a household are taken care of.

On a shorter-term basis, we see a major change taking place in higher education. A few years ago, the "in" thing in college was to major in a glamorous new field, such as marine biology, or highly academic subjects such as medieval history. In each case, one hundred students might be preparing for a career where only one job opening was likely to exist. A student preparing for what was considered to be a dull job in the business world was likely to experience derision, if not scorn, from fellow students and professors. In contrast, a swing aimed toward practical education has now been taking place.

The fastest-growing institution of higher education has been the two-year college, which stressed job-related courses. Particularly important is the growth of para-professional areas, such as dental, medical, and legal technology.

Burgeoning Service Businesses

A major phenomenon of recent years has been the much faster growth of the *service* area of the economy than the agricultural and manufacturing areas. Service businesses account for 50% of consumer dollars, and this percentage is growing every year. The productivity of lawyers, doctors, dentists, engineers, etc., can be increased greatly by intelligent use of para-professionals and computers to handle the more routine work. This trend is accelerating.

In the employment area, we see mixed trends developing. The job-seeker has a much more difficult task now than before. Many companies will deteriorate in the more difficult economy of the future. If employed by such a firm, the job-seeker will have neither job security nor opportunity.

It has been a common experience in the post-war period, for a college graduate to get a yearly salary increase, but find that the increase leaves him/her on merely the same level as what the newly graduated college student earns. During periods of economic prosperity, this is an encouragement to change jobs often. It becomes more risky however, during periods of high unemployment.

We would expect the most successful families to have multiple sources of income. Partly, this will consist of both parents working. In Scandinavian countries, where Socialism has reached an advanced stage, a woman who doesn't work is sometimes referred to as a "luxury wife." The main wage-earner of the family is also likely to have a second, part-time job, as has been true of many industrious Americans for many years.

Promising Outlook for Small Business

In our opinion, the opportunity for small, part-time business is and will continue to be great. Some of those businesses, started on a part-time basis, will eventually become large, striving enterprises. Larger companies are already over-burdened with government regulation, making it difficult to take advantage of new opportunities that arise. Caught in a profit squeeze, large companies will be divesting themselves of certain businesses which earn little or no profit, and are unrelated to their main business lines. These can be great opportunities for the alert entrepreneur. Often, the small business owner can make a good profit in these areas, simply by having lower overhead and greater flexibility in controlling costs.

Many Americans have had a kind of supplemental, part-time business for years, although they may not have realized it. They are "do-it-yourselfers." The main source of wealth accumulated by average Americans over the years has been their homes. This has been partly due to inflation of real estate values, but a great deal of it has been due to home improvements and/or home maintenance done by individuals themselves. In the last few years of escalating food prices, many families are also rediscovering the art of gardening. Maintaining and repairing the family car(s) has long been a favorite pastime of many Americans.

Barter

An interesting variation of "doing-it-yourself" is the bartering of services with others who have different skills. One person may be an amateur photographer, and another may be a do-it-yourselfer with carpentry skills. If each were to sell their product or service to the other, the proceeds from their efforts would be taxable. Technically, the bartering of services probably produces taxable income, particularly if the exchange is between strangers. However, everyday, millions of Americans exchange favors with each other, and even the most aggressive tax collector would probably not attempt to tax these transactions.

An acquaintance tells me of the financial difficulty of one of his employees when she left a small Virginia town to take a better-paying job in a medium-sized city. In her small town, her grandfather was a farmer, her father a retailer, her uncle a doctor, and her cousin an auto mechanic. Regardless of what she needed in her home town, she was able to obtain it at a discount, or at no charge. In turn, she had certain skills with which she had been able to help others. In her new job, she didn't have these opportunities for barter, even with a higher income.

Not only are Americans learning to tap new sources of income, but they are also becoming sharper consumers. They seek bargains and various creative ways to cut buying costs. When a person gets into the 50% tax bracket, a penny saved is equivalent to two cents earned.

The Real Cause of Inflation

Some Americans are becoming aware that the sole cause of inflation is the government. Through deficit spending and the pumping of more dollars into the money supply, the inevitable result is double-digit inflation, with the imminent threat of runaway inflation and economic collapse. I have spoken to survivors of Germany's inflation and collapse of the mark in the 1920's. All of them preferred living through the war under Hitler to the horror of the collapse of the currency, with the inherent problems of shortages and chaos.

Like an individual, the government cannot violate economic axioms with immunity. Government officials spend more than our tax money contributions, most of it in an irresponsible manner. Then because income is less than out-go, it cannot pay its bills. The government, however, unlike the people, has the power to print money. It merely prints more of it to cover deficit spending and national debt.

The United States was the founder of individual rights and its economic consequence — free enterprise. Because of this, we experienced the greatest economic progress and highest standard of living the world has known in the last two hundred years. Free enterprise is not only the most moral economic system, because it is consistent with human nature, it works. It is better than any system ever devised. This country's very foundations are, unfortunately, being threatened by politicians who do not understand free enterprise and are spending us into national bankruptcy.

Our schools are teaching our children that the free enterprise system does not work, that business men and women are evil, that the government can solve our problems, and that such socially-conscious jobs as welfare work are more "noble" than business careers.

I submit that if you wish to help your fellow human (and if you have some guts), the best way to do this is by starting your own business, the by-product of which is the creation of jobs. That is the best way to help any free individual.

Fortunately, there are a few pro-freedom individuals and business people. It is hoped that enough influence can be exercised by these people to persuade sufficient numbers of Americans to see the danger of current policies. The only solutions, as I see it, are in taking steps toward reducing the size and power of government, and the elimination of all laws that affect the marketplace. There is only one objective regulation of free markets — the law of supply and demand. The result would be not only fewer bankruptcies, but unprecedented material progress for us all.

ORDERING INFORMATION

The forms reproduced in this book have been supplied by Julius Blumberg, Inc., 66 White Street, New York, New York, 10013, and have been reprinted with permission.

For a complete fee schedule and list of available forms and kits, write directly to Julius Blumberg, Inc.

Appendices

APPENDIX I

Federal Court Listing — To file a bankruptcy action go to court nearest your residence. Addresses in phone book.

State	District	City
Alabama	Northern	Birmingham
	Middle	Montgomery
	Southern	Mobile
Alaska	—	Anchorage
Arizona	—	Phoenix
Arkansas	Eastern	Little Rock
	Western	Fort Smith
California	Northern	San Francisco
	Eastern	Sacramento
	Central	Los Angeles
	Southern	San Diego
Canal Zone, Panama	—	Ancon
Colorado	—	Denver
Connecticut	—	New Haven
Delaware	—	Wilmington
District of Columbia	—	Washington
Florida	Northern	Tallahassee
	Middle	Jacksonville
	Southern	Miami
Georgia	Northern	Atlanta
	Middle	Macon
	Southern	Savannah

State	District	City
Guam	—	Agana
Hawaii	—	Honolulu
Idaho	—	Boise
Illinois	Northern Eastern Southern	Chicago East St. Louis Peoria
Indiana	Northern Southern	Hammond Indianapolis
Iowa	Northern Southern	Cedar Rapids Des Moines
Kansas	—	Wichita
Kentucky	Eastern Western	Lexington Louisville
Louisiana	Eastern Western	New Orleans Shreveport
Maine	—	Portland
Maryland	—	Baltimore
Massachusetts	—	Boston
Michigan	Eastern Western	Detroit Grand Rapids
Minnesota	—	St. Paul
Mississippi	Northern Southern	Oxford Jackson
Missouri	Eastern Western	St. Louis Kansas City
Montana	—	Butte
Nebraska	—	Omaha
Nevada	—	Reno & Las Vegas
New Hampshire	—	Concord
New Jersey	—	Trenton
New Mexico	—	Albuquerque
New York	Northern Southern Eastern Western	Utica & Albany New York City Brooklyn Buffalo
North Carolina	Eastern Middle Western	Raleigh Greensboro Asheville

State	District	City
North Dakota	—	Fargo & Bismarck
Ohio	Northern Southern	Cleveland Columbus
Oklahoma	Northern Eastern Western	Tulsa Muskogee Oklahoma City
Oregon	—	Portland
Pennsylvania	Eastern Middle Western	Philadelphia Scranton Pittsburgh
Puerto Rico	—	San Juan
Rhode Island	—	Providence
South Carolina	—	Columbia
South Dakota	—	Sioux Falls
Tennessee	Eastern Middle Western	Knoxville Nashville Memphis
Texas	Northern Southern Eastern Western	Dallas Houston Tyler & Beaumont San Antonio
Utah	—	Salt Lake City
Vermont	—	Burlington
Virgin Islands	—	Charlotte Amalie
Virginia	Eastern Western	Norfolk Roanoke & Abingdon
Washington	Eastern Western	Spokane Seattle
West Virginia	Northern Southern	Elkins Charleston
Wisconsin	Eastern Western	Milwaukee Madison
Wyoming	—	Cheyenne

APPENDIX 2

Homestead Exemption Information (Excluded From Bankruptcy)

State	Amount	Who May Claim
Alabama	Area 160 acres. Value $2,000.	Any resident.
Alaska	Area 160 acres in country. ¼ acre in town or city, laid off in blocks or lots. Value not in excess of $19,000 for trailer or mobile home the exemption is $12,000.	Any resident who owns and uses same as his actual abode.
Arizona	In compact body. Residence and land of debtor not to exceed $20,000 in value, mobile home and land on which it is located not to exceed $10,000 in value. Claim for exemption must be filed in office of County Recorder.	Any person 18 or over married or single who resides in state.
Arkansas	In country, not over 160 acres. Value $2,500. Nor less than 80 acres regardless of value. In city, not over one acre and improvements. Same value as country, not to be reduced to less than ¼ acre regardless of value.	Resident married or head of family.
California	By any head of a family, of not exceeding $30,000 cash value, over and above all liens and encumbrances on the property at time of any levy of execution thereon; by any person 65 or older not exceeding $30,000 in cash value.	Resident head of family.
	By any other person, of not exceeding $15,000 in actual cash value, over all liens and encumbrances.	By any other resident
	House trailer or mobile home in which debtor or his family reside to maximum value of $15,000, over liens and encumbrances.	

State	Amount	Who May Claim
	Dwelling can include condominium or can be situated on property leased for a period of thirty years or more. Declaration must be recorded with county recorder.	
Colorado	No limitation on area. House and lots must not exceed $7,500 in value. Moveable structure to the extent of $5,000 if used and occupied as a place of residence by owner. Word "homestead" must be entered on margin of record title.	Householder, head of family.
Connecticut	No homestead exemption.	
Delaware	No homestead exemption.	
District of Columbia	No homestead exemption.	
Florida	160 acres in country, ½ acre in city. No limit on value may be claimed by recording declaration of homestead or after levy and before sale by ratifying officer who is to sell, in writing of claim of homestead. Interest in 98-year lease qualifies for Homestead exemption.	Head of family residing in state.
Georgia	Real estate not to exceed $500 in city or 50 acres in country with improvements, not to exceed $200. Includes specified personal property. Waiver note or written waiver if given contemporaneously with transaction would hold, but a sale or assignment of homestead has priority to ordinary waiver.	Head of family or aged or infirm person or one having care of dependent female of any age.
Hawaii	Any interest in one parcel of property owned by head of family or	Any person.

State	Amount	Who May Claim
	person 65 years or older may not exceed $30,000 when owned by any other person may not exceed $20,000 as determined by assessed valuation.	
Idaho	$10,000 where claimant is the head of family; $4,000 for any other person. Exemption is confined to dwelling house and land on which it is situated. Declaration must be executed and recorded.	Family. By any other person.
Illinois	$10,000 in land with buildings, owned or leased, occupied as residence.	Householder having a family.
Indiana	No homestead statute. Personal or family residence $5,000. Other real estate or tangible personal property $2,000. In no event shall total exemptions exceed $6,000. Wife can claim one-third of any real estate owned by husband.	Resident householder. Where a husband and wife are each conducting a separate and distinct business each may have the full exemption of $1,000.
Iowa	If within city or town plot must not exceed one-half acre, otherwise not more than 40 acres, but if in either case value is less than $500, it may be enlarged to reach that amount. Exceptions: Homestead liable for deficiency remaining after exhausting all other nonexempt property where debt is contracted prior to acquisition of homestead; by written contract stipulating that homestead shall be liable, also, for debts incurred for work done or material furnished exclusively for the improvement of homestead; also, if no survivor or issue, for payment of debts to	Resident, head of family, husband or wife.

State	Amount	Who May Claim
	which it might at that time be subject if it had never been held as a homestead.	
Kansas	160 acres, farm; 1 acre in city, occupied as residence.	Any resident.
Kentucky	$1,000, unless liability existed before purchase of land. Mortgage on homestead, release or waiver must be in writing and signed also by wife and recorded.	Householder.
Louisiana	$15,000 not over 160 acres. Exemption may be waived. Claim must be in writing and recorded in parish where homestead is situated.	Resident with family or other dependents.
Maine	$5,000 if declaration is filed with registry of deeds. The term "homestead" includes a mobile home used by the householder as principal residence.	Householder.
Maryland	None.	
Massachusetts	$24,000 in value of land or buildings. Must be established by deed or declaration and recorded. Provisions for family not exceeding $300 in value, and sewing machine not over $200 in value.	Householder who has family, and real estate serves as the principal residence of debtor and family.
Michigan	$3,500 in lot, if in city, and not exceeding 40 acres in extent, if in country.	Resident citizen.
Minnesota	80 acres in country, in village or city ½ acre with improvements.	Resident.
Mississippi	$15,000 in value and not exceeding 160 acres if outside city, town	Citizen householder with family. Husband

State	Amount	Who May Claim
	or village. Homestead can be house or apartment or condominium. Homestead exemption is denied under certain circumstances where portions of property are rented or used for other commercial purposes.	or wife, widow or widower without a family, or not occupying homestead, if over 60 years of age, who has been an exemptionship.
Missouri	In country, 160 acres, value $1,500. In cities and towns, $1,500 to $3,000, depending on population. Area in cities and towns also depends on population.	Head of family.
Montana	Not exceeding $7,500 assessed valuation on 320 acres of agricultural land or ¼ acre in city.	Resident head of family. Resident single person over 60 years.
Nebraska	$4,000, consisting of dwelling in which claimant lives and its appurtenances, not over 160 acres in country; 2 adjoining lots in city.	Head of family.
Nevada	$25,000 but does not apply in claim for purchase price, taxes on property or lien of mortgage or deed of trust created by and with the consent of the husband and wife. Declaration of homestead must be recorded with County Recorder. Mortgage or conveyance of homestead property invalid, unless signature of husband and wife be obtained to same and instrument be acknowledged by wife separately and apart from husband.	Any head of family or husband or wife or single person.
New Hampshire	$2,500.	Debtor, wife and children of debtor.

State	Amount	Who May Claim
New Jersey	No statutory provisions.	
New Mexico	$10,000.	Husband and wife or widow or widower living with unmarried daughter or minor son or person supporting himself.
New York	Lot of land with dwelling owned and occupied as a principal residence, not to exceed $10,000 in value above liens.	Resident householder or woman, principal residence only.
North Carolina	$1,000.	Resident.
North Dakota	Resident land and dwelling house with improvements, not to exceed $60,000 over and above liens.	Resident head of family.
Ohio	$5,000.	Husband and wife living together, a widow or a widower living with an unmarried daughter or unmarried minor son.
Oklahoma	100% including household and kitchen furniture.	Resident head of family.
Oregon	Not over $12,000 and not exceeding one block in any town or city laid off into blocks and lots; not exceeding 160 acres elsewhere. Mobile home, $12,000. Proceeds of sale exempt for one year if to be used to purchase another homestead.	Resident householder.
Pennsylvania	None.	
Rhode Island	None.	

State	Amount	Who May Claim
South Carolina	$1,000 and yearly products. Waiver of unassigned homestead invalid, except by deed or mortgage. No limitation in area.	Head of family.
South Dakota	A homestead is absolutely exempt. If property is sold, then proceeds up to $30,000 will be exempt for one year from receipt thereof.	Head of family, or in case he fails to claim, any member of the family over 14 years of age.
Tennessee	$1,000.	Resident head of family.
Texas	Homestead for a family, if not in a city, town or village, not more than 200 acres; single person not in a city, town or village not more than 100 acres; for family or single person in city, town or village lot or lots not to exceed $10,000 in value.	Head of family.
Utah	$6,000 and $2,000 in addition for wife, also $800 additional for each member of the family.	Head of family.
Vermont	The homestead of a natural person consisting of a dwelling house, outbuildings and the land used in connection therewith, not exceeding $5,000 in value, and owned and used or kept by such person as a homestead together with the rents, issues, profits and products thereof.	Housekeeper or head of a family.
Virginia	An estate not in excess of $5,000 comprised of personal and real property of debtor.	Resident householder or head of family.
Washington	Not exceeding $20,000. Consists of dwelling house with pertinent	Resident head of family.

State	Amount	Who May Claim
	buildings and land or land with improvements purchased with the intention of building a house and residing therein. May be selected at any time before sale by filing declaration with county auditor. Not exempt from claims of mechanic's, laborer's or materialmen's liens or from mortgages.	
West Virginia	$1,000. Claim to be executed and recorded.	Husbands, parents, or infants of deceased or insane parents.
Wisconsin	$25,000. Consists of dwelling house and its appurtenances. Not exceeding 4 acres and not less than ¼ acre.	Resident.
Wyoming	$6,000. House and lot or lots in city, on farm consisting of any number of acres within the value limitation. Must be occupied by owner or his family. Creditor may bring proceeding if he believes property worth over $6,000. On sale, if it brings less, creditor liable for expenses.	Householder, being head of family and every resident 60 years or over wehther head of family or not. Widow, husband or minor child entitled to homestead on death of owner, subject to debts of deceased.

Reprinted from the *Credit Manual of Commercial Laws*, 1979, National Association of Credit Management, New York, New York.

APPENDIX 3

Personal Property Exemptions

State:	Alabama
Amount:	$1,000 and necessary family clothing, family portraits and books. Personal property in the custody of a trustee in the custody of a trustee in bankruptcy is exempt to the bankrupt and cannot be garnished. Insurance for benefit of wife and children to extent of premium of $1,000 per year.
Who May Claim:	Any resident.
Wages*:	Of laborers or employees residents of the State in an amount equal to 75% of wages. On judgments based on consumer transactions greater of 80% of weekly disposable earnings per week exceed 50 times federal minimum hourly wage.

State:	Alaska
Amount:	Miscellaneous personal property, furnishings, and utensils to value of $1,200. Tools, implements, etc. to carry on trade or profession to the value of $2,500. Debtor must designate article for which he claims exemption at the time of levy of exemption. No articles are exempt from execution on a judgment recovered for the purchase price of same.
Who May Claim:	Any resident.
Wages:	25% of disposable income for week or amount of $114 of weekly income, whichever is less.

*Title III of the Federal Consumer Credit Protection Act exempts from garnishment the greater of 75% of disposable earnings per work week or an amount each week equal to 30 times the Federal minimum hourly wage. The exemption does not apply to support orders or orders of any court of bankruptcy. The statute does not provide that an employee cannot be discharged because his earnings have been subjected to garnishment for one indebtedness. State laws providing lesser limitations are superseded by the Federal law.

Reprinted from the *Credit Manual of Commerical Laws*, 1979, National Association of Credit Management, New York, New York.

Personal Property Exemptions

State:	Arizona
Amount:	Property must be designated by debtor. Household goods, artisans' tools, professional man's equipment, various farm implements, and miscellaneous articles. Money received by surviving spouse or child upon life of deceased spouse or parent not exceeding $10,000.
Who May Claim:	Every family.
Wages:	One-half of earnings for 30 days prior to levy when necessary for use of family.

State:	Arkansas
Amount:	Specific articles not exceeding $200 in addition to wearing apparel. Articles with value of $500 besides clothes.
Who May Claim:	Resident who is not married or head of family. Married or head of family.
Wages:	Constitutional exemption: Single person—$200 including personal property other than wearing apparel. Head of family—$500 including personal property other than wearing apparel. Laborers and Mechanics—Wages for 60 days exempt provided statement is filed.

State:	California
Amount:	Numerous necessary articles for their business, trade, calling, profession, etc., up to $2,500 over and above all encumbrances on the property and household furniture and equipment. Motor vehicle to value above encumbrances on the vehicle provided that the value of the vehicle shall not exceed $500, or as set forth in Used Car Guide or if not set forth $1,000, house trailer occupied by debtor family to value of $9,500 above all encumbrances on the house trailer. Relocation payments for a period of six months.
Who May Claim:	Any person. Farmers, mechanics, miners, truckmen, professional men, etc.
Wages:	Greater of 50% or portion exempt by federal statute of the earnings of the defendant or judgment debtor received for his personal services rendered at any time within thirty days next preceding the levy of attachment or execution. All of such earnings, if necessary for the use of the debtor's family, residing in this State, and supported in whole or in part by such debtor unless the debts are: (a) In-

Personal Property Exemptions

	curred by such debtor, his wife or family, for the common necessaries of life: or (b) Incurred for personal services rendered by any such employee, or former employee, of such debtor.
State:	Colorado
Amount:	Necessary wearing apparel for each head of family, single person and dependent to the extent of $400 per person; watches, jewelry and articles of adornment of each head of family, single person and dependent $100 per person; library, family pictures and school books of head of family and dependents to the extent of $500, single person to the extent of $200; burial sites; household goods to the extent of $1,000 in value for head of family and $400 for a single person; provisions and fuel on hand for use head of family and dependents to the extent of $300, for a single person $100; every head of family engaged in agriculture, livestock not exceeding $2,000 and horses, mules, carts, machinery not exceeding $1,500, in the case of a single person, $1,000 and $750 respectively; pensions or compensations as a result of service in the Armed Forces; stock in trade, supplies, fixtures, tools of business not exceeding $750; motor vehicle not exceeding $500; library of a professional person not exceeding $750; life insurance policies to the extent of $5,000; house trailer to the extent of $2,500 while occupied as a place of residence by head of the family; aggregate value of all items excepted shall be limited to $12,500.
Who May Claim:	Single resident or head of family.
Wages:	Greater of 75% of disposable earnings per week of amount in which disposable earnings exceed 30 times federal minimum hourly wage for debts arising from consumer credit sales. *Head of family* — 70% of earnings due at time of service. *Single person* — 35% of earnings due at time of service.
State:	Connecticut
Amount:	Certain specific articles such as apparel, household furniture entirely exempt, and other articles up to designated values.
Who May Claim:	Resident

Personal Property Exemptions

Wages:	Greater of 75% of disposable earnings per week up to amount equal to 40 times Federal minimum hourly wage. SUPPORT ORDERS — $70 per week exempt on court order for support of wife and children.

State:	Delaware
Amount:	Books, pictures, church pew, burial lot, wearing apparel of family, sewing machines, implements of trade not exceeding $75 in New Castle, Sussex counties and $50 in Kent County. General exemption of personal property — New Castle County $200, Kent County $150.
Who May Claim:	Any resident. Any resident being head of family.
Wages:	Exemption of 85% of wages. Support orders — 75% of net wages exempt on order for support of one child reduced by 5% for each additional child.

State:	District of Columbia
Amount:	Implements and tools to extent of $200. Household furniture, etc., to value of $300; also certain miscellaneous articles. Wearing apparel.
Who May Claim:	Resident head of family or householder. All persons.
Wages:	Greater of 75% of disposable earnings per week or amount of disposable earnings per week equal to 30 times Federal minimum hourly wage. *Withholding by Garnishee-Employer* — 90% of first $200 of gross wages payable in a month, 80% of gross wages payable in a month in excess of $200 and under $500. Calendar month consists of 4-1/3 workweeks. *Debtor Principal Support of Family* —$200 each month of earnings other than wages of resident or non-resident earning major portion of livelihood in D.C. exempt for two months preceding issuance of writ. *Debtor Not Principal Support of Family* — $60 each month is exempt. Support judgments 50% of gross wages exempt.

State:	Florida
Amount:	Cash surrender value of life insurance policy. Proceeds of the life insurance of person dying within state. Proceeds of disability insurance unless taken out for benefit of creditors. Other articles up to designated value.
Who May Claim:	Head of family residing in state.

Personal Property Exemptions

Wages:	Entire wages of the head of family when wages are due for personal labor or services of such person. Amount exempt is exclusive of payroll deductions for taxes.
State:	Georgia
Amount:	Value at $1,600, real or personal or both, set apart by petition. Purchase money debt enforceable against. (Either this exemption or homestead exemption may be claimed but not both.)
Who May Claim:	Head of family or aged or infirm person or one having care of dependent female of any age.
Wages:	Greater of 75% of disposable earnings per week or amount by which disposable earnings exceed 30 times the federal minimum hourly wage.
State:	Hawaii
Amount:	Various specified articles of personal property. (The exemption does not apply, however, to execution on a judgment recovered for the purchase price of such goods as on a foreclosure of a mortgage on the goods.)
Who May Claim:	Any resident.
Wages:	95% of first $100, 90% of next $100 and 80% of disposable wages in excess of $200 per month or equivalent per week.
State:	Idaho
Amount:	Burial plot, necessary health aids, public assistance benefits, health benefits—100% exemption; if necessary for support: income of various types and some assets—100% exemption; necessary furnishings and appliances, personal clothing, books, musical instruments, animals, family portraits and heirlooms—value not to exceed $500; personal jewelry—value not to exceed $250; implements, professional books, tools of the trade—value not to exceed $1000; 1 motor vehicle—value not to exceed $500; various other types of property.
Who May Claim:	Actual resident.
Wages:	Greater of 75% of disposable earnings for workweek or amount each week equal to 30 times federal minimum hourly wage.

Personal Property Exemptions

State:	Illinois
Amount:	Wearing apparel, Bible, school books, family pictures, military pensions for 1 year, $300, plus $700 if head of family with whom he lives.
Who May Claim:	Any person.
Wages:	Greater of 15% of gross wages or amount of weekly disposable wages not in excess of 30 times federal minimum hourly wage. Includes compensation by commissions, bonuses and periodic payments from retirement or pension funds.

State:	Indiana
Amount:	Tangible personal property, along with other non-residential personal property, not to exceed $2,000. Intangible personal property, including choses in action (but excluding debts owing, and income owing) up to $100.
Who May Claim:	Debtor residing in state. Where a husband and wife are each conducting a separate & distinct business out of their own individual funds each may claim separate exemption.
Wages:	UCCC provides exemption for 75% of disposable earnings per week in excess of 30 times Federal minimum hourly wage. The following provisions have not been repealed by the UCCC and appear to be in conflict with it: Householder exemption not exceeding $25, resident householder $15 per week plus 90% of excess over $15 exempt as to claims arising out of contract, $1,000 maximum. In *Mins v. Consumer Credit Corp.*, (Ind. Sup. Ct., March 13, 1974), the court held that statute most beneficial to householder would be enforced.

State:	Iowa
Amount:	Wearing apparel, books, pictures or musical instruments, certain livestock, food for six months, kitchen furniture not to exceed $200. Tools, equipment, books, etc. used in trade or profession, limited number of farm animals. Wearing apparel and trunk to contain same. Proceeds of life insurance.
Who May Claim:	Resident, head of family. Non-resident or unmarried resident not head of family.

Personal Property Exemptions

Wages:	75% of disposable earnings for week or amount by which disposable earnings for week exceed 30 times federal minimum hourly wage, whichever is greater. Maximum amount that can be garnished in any year is $250 for each creditor.

State:	Kansas
Amount:	Head of household: (1) Furnishing and supplies, including food & clothing for a period of 1 year; (2) one means of conveyance; (3) family burial plot; (4) equipment or other means of production necessary in carrying on a trade, business, occupation or profession not to exceed $5,000. Not head of household: (1) Personal clothing; (2) equipment or other means of production necessary in carrying on a trade, business, occupation or profession not to exceed $2,000.
Who May Claim:	Resident, head of family. Any resident.
Wages:	75% of disposable earnings for week or amount by which disposable earnings exceed 30 times Federal minimum hourly wage, whichever is greater. For support orders: 40% of weekly disposable earnings or 50% if debtor is supporting a spouse or child not involved in the support order; exemption is reduced by 5% if garnishment is necessary to enforce a support order issued more than 12 weeks prior to the workweek.

State:	Kentucky
Amount:	Many articles, household good, wearing apparel, etc., not to exceed $1,500 in value, mechanic's tools, livestock not to exceed $1,500 in value; one motor vehicle not to exceed $1,500 in value if used by person engaged in farming or who uses vehicle in his employment, library of professional men, etc.
Who May Claim:	Resident with a family.
Wages:	Greater of 75% of disposable income per week or amount by which disposable earnings exceed 30 times Federal minimum hourly wage. Exemptions inapplicable to support orders.

State:	Louisiana
Amount:	Certain articles specified in statute, such as clothing, tools of a trade and other articles.

Personal Property Exemptions

Who May Claim:	Householder.
Wages:	75% of disposable earnings for any week, but not less than 30 times the Federal minimum hourly wage in effect when the wages are payable.

State:	Maine
Amount:	Debtor's apparel, household furniture necessary for the family not exceeding $1,000 in value; radio and one television not exceeding $200 in value; automobile or truck not exceeding $1,000 in value; family portraits, Bibles and school books in actual use and library not to exceed $150 in value; watch not exceeding $50 in value; wedding ring and engagement ring not exceeding in $200 in value; interest in church pew; one cooking stove, iron stove, charcoal not exceeding 12 cords of wood; anthracite coal not exceeding five tons; bituminous coal not exceeding 50 bushels; $50 worth of lumber; heating gas not exceeding $200; farm produce until harvested one barrel of flour, 50 bushels of oats, 50 barrels of potatoes, corn and grain not exceeding 30 bushels; food necessary for family and debtor; tools necessary for his trade or occupation not exceeding $1,000 in value; one sewing machine, one refrigerator, one washing machine not exceeding $200 in value; a pair of working cattle or mules, two horses not exceeding $400 in value; domestic fowl not exceeding $100 in value; specified farm equipment; boat not exceeding two tons used in fishing business.
Who May Claim:	Resident.
Wages:	Greater of 75% of disposable earnings for week or amount by which disposable earnings exceed 30 times federal minimum hourly wage. 40 times the hourly wage in consumer transactions. Wages due debtor for wife's or minor child's personal service are exempt. Trustee process—100% of wages exempt.

State:	Maryland
Amount:	(1) $500 real or personal property now exempt (no more than $200 in cash). (2) Or certain household goods.
Who May Claim:	Bona fide residents.
Wages:	Wages — $120 exempt multiplied by the number of weeks in which such wages due were earned or 75% of such wages, whichever is greater. Except that in Caroline,

Personal Property Exemptions

Worchester, Kent and Queen Anne counties exemption for any workweek shall be greater of 75% of wages due or 30 times Federal minimum hourly wage.

State: Massachusetts

Amount: Many articles. Household furniture not exceeding $3,000 in value. Materials and stock necessary for carrying on trade or business, value of $500. Cash savings or deposits not to exceed $80. An automobile necessary for personal transportation or to secure or maintain employment, not exceeding $700.

Who May Claim: Resident.

Wages: Wages for personal labor or services exempted from attachment to amount of $125 per week. Exemption of $75 of personal income which is not otherwise exempt by law.

State: Michigan

Amount: As to householders: certain articles, household goods, amounting to $1,000. As to businessmen: tools, implements, stock in trade necessary to carry on business, $1,000. Partners' right in specific partnership property is not subject to attachment or execution except on a claim against the partnership. When partnership debt there is no exemption under the laws.

Who May Claim: Resident citizen.

Wages: Householder with family — 60% exemption with following limitations: On first garnishment, maximum $50 per week and minimum $30 per week for labor of one week. For more than one week's labor, maximum $90 and minimum $60. As to subsequent garnishments for one week's labor, maximum per week is $60 and minimum $24. For a period of more than 16 days, maximum is $60 and minimum $30. Employee not householder with family — First garnishment 40% exemption, with $50 maximum and $20 minimum. In other cases 30% or $20 maximum and $10 minimum.

State: Minnesota

Amount: Farm machines and implements and livestock produce and standing crops not exceeding $5,000 in value; tools and stock of a trade or business not exceeding $5,000 in value except that the total of all of the above shall not

Personal Property Exemptions

	exceed $5,000; clothes, household furniture, etc., not exceeding $3,000 in value; other specific articles; a mobile home, the earnings of a minor child of any debtor by reason of any liability of any such debtor not contracted for the special benefit of said child. Nothing exempt from execution or attachment in action for balance of purchase price thereof.
Who May Claim:	Resident.
Wages:	"Seventy-five percent of disposable earnings or 40 times the federal minimum hourly wage times the number of work weeks in the pay period, whichever is greater." Where debtor has been on relief, exemption for a period of 6 months from date of return to private employment.
State:	Mississippi
Amount.	Tools, equipment, etc., used in connection with trade or profession; the books of a student, wearing apparel of every person, libraries of all persons, including books, drawings and paintings, not exceeding $1,200 in value and other specified articles. Specified articles of farm equipment animals and produce, plus household and kitchen, not exceeding in value $1,200 and all family portraits.
Who May Claim:	Any person. Head of family.
Wages:	75% of wages or salaries of resident laborer or employee.
State:	Missouri
Amount:	Head of family: wearing apparel, family books, furniture worth not more than $200, food not worth more than $200, assorted animals, books, tools of the trade or $500 lump sum in lieu of all the above. Non-head of family: wearing apparel and tools of the trade.
Who May Claim:	Head of family. Non-head of family.
Wages:	Greatest of (1) 75% of workweek earnings, (2) weekly amount equal to 30 times federal minimum hourly wage.
State:	Montana
Amount:	Special articles, including household goods, and tools to carry on business. One automobile or truck value of $300. Proceeds of life insurance purchased with premiums not exceeding $500 per year. Professional libraries. Miner

Personal Property Exemptions

	entitled to $1,000. Only wearing apparel to unmarried person under 60 years. Non resident not entitled to exemption.
Who May Claim:	Resident head of family. Resident single person over 60 years.
Wages:	All wages for 45 days preceding garnishment if necessary for support of family. If debt incurred for gasoline or common necessities then only 50% is exempt.

State:	Nebraska
Amount:	Personal possessions of debtor and family; necessary wearing apparel of debtor and family; kitchen utensils and household furniture selected by debtor to $1,500; equipment or tools not exceeding $1,500; provisions for debtor and family necessary for 6 months' support; and fuel necessary for 6 months. All articles intended to be exempt shall be chosen by debtor, his agent or legal rep.; pension of soldier and sailor and property purchased therewith $2,000; life insurance on policies not payable to executor or administrator of insured or his beneficiary in an amount paid for by annual premium not exceeding $500.
Who May Claim:	Any resident debtor.
Wages:	Greatest of 75% of disposable earnings or amount equal to 30 times Federal minimum hourly wage or 85% of disposable earnings if wage earner is head of family.

State:	Nevada
Amount:	Private libraries over $500; family fixtures and keepsakes; necessary household goods, appliances and furniture not over $1,000; farm trucks, farm stocks, farm tools, supplies and seed not over $1,500; tools, instruments and materials used to carry on the trade not over $1,500; dwelling of a miner or prospector not over $500; also cars and appliances necessary to carry on mining operations not over $500; mining claim actually worked by bankrupt not over $1,000; one vehicle not over $1,000 if necessary for occupation or profession of debtor; poultry not over $80; fire engines, hooks and ladders and apparatus of fire company; all arms, uniforms required by law to be kept by debtor plus one gun selected by debtor; all court houses, jails and property related thereto; all monies growing out of any life insurance if annual

Personal Property Exemptions

	premium paid not over $500; homestead as provided by law; dwelling of judgment debtor occupied as home for himself and family, not over $10,000 in value, if dwelling is not on lands owned by debtor.
Who May Claim:	Any head of family or husband or wife or single person.
Wages:	The greater of 75% of disposable earnings or the amount by which disposable earnings exceed 30 times the minimum hourly Federal wage law. Exemption does not apply to support orders.
State:	New Hampshire
Amount:	Household furniture $1,000; wearing apparel and tools in trade to value of $600. Also miscellaneous property set forth in statute.
Who May Claim:	Debtor.
Wages:	Wages for labor performed after service of writ; wages for labor performed before service exempt unless action founded on debt on judgment issued by state court. In such case wages equal to 50 times Federal minimum hourly wage are exempt. Special exemption for small loan law debts.
State:	New Jersey
Amount:	Personal Property, value $1,000, and wearing apparel.
Who May Claim:	Head of resident family.
Wages:	Minimum exemption of $48 per week; 90% exemption if earnings are $7,500 per year or less. If earnings are more than $7,500 reduced exemption percentage by order of court.
State:	New Mexico
Amount:	Wearing apparel, household goods under certain values. Many specified articles. $500 real or personal property exclusive of articles specified if debtor has no homestead, unless debt is for necessaries or for manual labor. Resident not having household has additional exemption of $1,000 of personal property. Personal property used as security under UCC is not exempt.
Who May Claim:	Resident. There are some minor differences for a non-head of household.

Personal Property Exemptions

Wages:	Greater of 75% of debtor's disposable earnings or of excess of 40 times Federal minimum hourly wage rate. Disposable earnings is that part of debtor's salary remaining after deduction of amounts required to be withheld by law.

State:	New York
Amount:	All wearing apparel, household goods, tools, implements to the value of $600. Certain other articles.
Who May Claim:	Householder or woman. Male person, not householder, has similar exemption ($450) not including household furniture.
Wages:	Earnings of $85 or less per week are entirely exempt; and 90% of earnings for services within 60 days before and any time after income execution; exemption may be reduced by amount court determines unnecessary for reasonable requirements of debtor and dependents.

State:	North Carolina
Amount:	$500 in property to be selected by owner.
Who May Claim:	Resident.
Wages:	Earnings for personal services for 60 days preceding levy if necessary for support of family.

State:	North Dakota
Amount:	Head of a family, money or personal property $2,000; single person, money or personal property, $150. All wearing apparel and clothing of the debtor and his family or one year's provisions and fuel and crops raised by him on an area not to exceed 160 acres occupied as his homestead.
Who May Claim:	Head of a family or single person.
Wages:	Greater of 75% of debtor's disposable earnings or of excess of 40 times Federal minimum hourly wage rate. 100% of earnings for personal services within 60 days can be exempted by judge upon affidavit of need for support of family.

State:	Ohio
Amount:	Certain specified articles, including wearing apparel, tools and implements for carrying out profession, trade or business and a portion of personal earnings for services

Personal Property Exemptions

	rendered within 30 days before the issuing of the attachment. The dollar amounts of these articles are greater in the case of a head of a family.
Who May Claim:	Resident.
Wages:	75% of disposable earnings for week or excess of 30 times Federal minimum hourly wage, whichever is greater.
State.	Oklahoma
Amount:	Numerous articles, household furniture, books, pictures, wearing apparel, specified animals, tools, etc. Motor vehicle of a value not to exceed $1,500 for head of family.
Who May Claim:	Resident.
Wages:	75% of all earnings for personal or professional services earned during the 90 days before execution. Garnishment to satisfy child support order may, in certain cases, extend to 33-1/3% of debtors wages. Earnings for personal services are 100% exempt from garnishment prior to trial court judgment with statutory exceptions.
State:	Oregon
Amount:	Books, pictures, musical instruments $150; wearing apparel $500; household goods, furniture and radio $800; domestic animals $600; tools, library, etc., necessary to carry on trade or profession except for payment of debt, contracted to assist in carrying on trade or profession $1,600; vehicle $800; vehicle necessary to carry on trade or business may not exceed $1,600. No article is exempt from execution on judgment recovered for its purchase price.
Who May Claim:	Householder.
Wages:	Greater of 75% of disposable earnings for week or amount by which disposable earnings exceed 40 times the Federal minimum hourly wage.
State:	Pennsylvania
Amount:	$300 in real or personal property, also sewing machines, wearing apparel, other specified articles and certain leased articles.
Who May Claim:	Resident.
Wages:	100% of all wages; does not apply to support orders.

Personal Property Exemptions

State:	Rhode Island
Amount:	Wearing apparel, household goods to value of $1,000, tools used in trade to value of $500. Certain personal property of a housekeeper not exceeding $1,000.
Who May Claim:	Resident.
Wages:	Not exceeding $50.
State:	South Carolina
Amount:	$500, not to apply on articles upon which judgment was obtained. Clothes, tools for trade, value $300. Partner entitled to exemption against individual creditors out of his partnership interest.
Who May Claim:	Head of family. Persons not head of family.
Wages:	100% of earnings for personal services.
State:	South Dakota
Amount:	$1,500 to head of family, $900 to person not head of family. Both of the above are in addition to what are known as absolute exemptions.
Who May Claim:	Debtor, his agent or attorney, head of family or in case of his failure to do so by any member of his family over the age of 14 years.
Wages:	100% of earnings for personal services within 60 days if necessary for support of family.
State:	Tennessee
Amount:	Personal property up to $1,500. Residents are entitled to absolute exemption on necessary and proper wearing apparel of debtor and his family, family portraits, Bible and school books.
Who May Claim:	All persons who are bona fide citizens and permanent residents of Tennessee.
Wages:	Greater of 75% of disposable earnings per week or amount by which disposable earnings exceed 30 times the Federal minimum hourly wage (does not apply to child support orders or to alimony to unmarried spouse); additional $2.50 per week exemption for each resident, dependent child under 16.
State:	Texas
Amount:	Personal property not to exceed an aggregate fair market value of $15,000 for each single adult person and $30,000

Personal Property Exemptions

	for a family which can include the following: furnishings of a home; all the following implements necessary for farming or ranching: tools, equipment, books used in trade or profession, wearing apparel, firearms, athletic and sporting equipment. Any two of the following means of travel: two animals, a saddle and bridle for each: horses, colts, mules, donkeys, bicycle or motorcycle, wagon, cart or dray, automobile, station wagon, truck trailer, camper truck, truck, pick-up truck; livestock and fowl not to exceed the following in number and forage on hand reasonably necessary for their consumption: five cows and their calves, one breeding age bull, 20 hogs, 20 sheet, 20 goats, 50 chickens, 30 turkeys, 30 ducks, 30 geese, 30 guineas; dog, cat and other household pets.
Who May Claim:	Every family.
Wages:	Current wages.

State:	Utah
Amount:	Specified articles such as furniture up to $300 and tools or implements of trade to $500. In addition a surviving spouse of a domiciled debtor is entitled to $3,500.00 from the estate and household furniture, automobile, furnishings, appliances and personal effects. If no surviving spouse, children entitled to same property. In addition, the surviving spouse and minor children are entitled to allowance from the estate for maintenance during the period of administration.
Who May Claim:	Head of family.
Wages:	Married man or head of family one-half of earnings for 30 days prior to levy if head of family and his earnings are necessary for their support. Minimum exemption of $50 per month. Judgments arising from debts on consumer credit sales greater of 75% of disposable earnings per week or 40 times Federal minimum hourly wage.

State:	Vermont
Amount:	Specified articles. Specified professional books, clergyman, physician, dentist and lawyer value $200.
Who May Claim:	Resident.
Wages:	75% of disposable earnings for week or excess of 30 times Federal minimum hourly wage whichever is greater. Different formula for child support orders.

Personal Property Exemptions

State:	Virginia
Amount:	In addition to the $5,000 estate, enumerated articles such as the family Bible, wedding rings, wearing apparel, furniture, etc.
Who May Claim:	Resident householder or head of family.
Wages:	75% of disposable earnings for that week or of excess of 30 times Federal minimum hourly wage, whichever is greater. For support orders: 40% of weekly disposable earnings or 50% if debtor is supporting a spouse or dependent child not involved in the support order. Exemption is reduced by 5% if garnishment is necessary to enforce a support order issued more than 12 weeks prior to the beginning of the work week.

State:	Washington
Amount:	Household furniture and utensils, $1,000. $400 of other goods (no more than $100 in cash), wearing apparel, but not to exceed $500 in value of furs, jewelry and personal items. Many specially enumerated articles. Pension and life insurance also exempt.
Who May Claim:	Householder in case of household furniture. Beneficiary in case of pensions and life insurance.
Wages:	The greater part of 40 times the state hourly minimum wage or of 75% of the disposable earnings of the defendant is exempt from garnishment. Disposable earnings means that part of the earnings remaining after deduction of the amounts required by law to be withheld.

State:	West Virginia
Amount:	$1,000 for husband, parent residing in state, infant children of deceased parents. Many special articles. $50 worth of tools or implements.
Who May Claim:	Resident and head of family only.
Wages:	80% of wages due or to become due within one year after issuance of execution. $20 per week minimum.

State:	Wisconsin
Amount:	Automobiles used and kept for purpose of carrying on debtor's business to value of $1,000. Small tools and implements not exceeding $200 in value, and one tractor worth $1,500. Apparel not to exceed $400 and furniture up to $200.

Personal Property Exemptions

Who May Claim:	Resident. Mechanic, artisan or laborer.
Wages:	Greater of 75% of debtor's disposable earnings or of excess of 30 times Federal minimum hourly wage rate. Disposable earnings means that part of earnings after deduction of amounts required by law to be withheld. Employee with dependents — basic exemption of $120 plus $20 per dependent for each 30 day period prior to service of process, maximum exemption 75% of income. Employee without dependents — basic exemption of 60% of income for each 30 day period prior to service of process. Minimum $75, maximum $100.

State:	Wyoming
Amount:	Bible, pictures, school books, lot in cemetery, furniture, provisions, household articles, value $1,000, clothing value $400. Tools, teams, implements, stock in trade to carry on business not over $1,000 and library, instruments and implements, $1,000.
Who May Claim:	Head of family or person 60 years or over residing in state. Every resident. Professional men.
Wages:	Judgements on consumer credit sales, home or loan; greater of 75% of disposable earnings or excess over 30 times Federal minimum wage. Otherwise, 50% of earnings for personal services within 60 days before levy if necessary for use of resident family.

APPENDIX 4

UNITED STATES BANKRUPTCY COURT FOR THE DISTRICT OF

In re

Debtor

Include here all names used by debtor within last 6 years.

CASE NO.

STATEMENT OF FINANCIAL AFFAIRS FOR DEBTOR ENGAGED IN BUSINESS

Each question should be answered or the failure to answer explained. If the answer is "none," this should be stated. If additional space is needed for the answer to any question, a separate sheet, properly identified, and made part hereof, should be used and attached.

If the debtor is a partnership or a corporation, the questions shall be deemed to be addressed to, and shall be answered on behalf of, the partnership or corporation; and the statement shall be certified by a member of the partnership or by a duly authorized officer of the corporation.

The term, "original petition," as used in the following questions, shall mean the petition filed under Rule 1002, 1003, or 1004.

(If this form is used by joint debtors wherever the word "debtor" or words referring to debtor are used they shall be read as if in the plural.)

1. Nature, location, and name of business.

a. Under what name and where do you carry on your business?

b. In what business are you engaged?
(If business operations have been terminated, give the date of such termination.)

c. When did you commence such business?

d. Where else, and under what other names, have you carried on business within the 6 years immediately preceding the filing of the original petition herein?
(Give street addresses, the names of any partners, joint adventurers, or other associates, the nature of the business, and the periods for which it was carried on.)

e. What is your employer identification number? Your social security number?

2. Books and records.

a. By whom, or under whose supervision, have your books of account and records been kept during the 2 years immediately preceding the filing of the original petition herein?
(Give names, addresses, and periods of time.)

b. By whom have your books of account and records been audited during the 2 years immediately preceding the filing of the original petition herein?
(Give names, addresses, and dates of audits.)

c. In whose possession are your books of account and records?
(Give names and addresses.)

d. If any of these books or records are not available, explain.

e. Have any books of account or records relating to your affairs been destroyed, lost, or otherwise disposed of within the 2 years immediately preceding the filing of the original petition herein?
(If so, give particulars, including date of destruction, loss, or disposition, and reason therefor.)

3. Financial statements.

Have you issued any written financial statements within the 2 years immediately preceding the filing of the original petition herein?
(Give dates, and the names and addresses of the persons to whom issued, including mercantile and trade agencies.)

4. Inventories.

a. When was the last inventory of your property taken?

b. By whom, or under whose supervision, was this inventory taken?

c. What was the amount, in dollars, of the inventory?
(State whether the inventory was taken at cost, market, or otherwise.)

d. When was the next prior inventory of your property taken?

e. By whom, or under whose supervision, was this inventory taken?

f. What was the amount, in dollars, of the inventory?
(State whether the inventory was taken at cost, market, or otherwise.)

g. In whose possession are the records of the 2 inventories above referred to?
(Give names and addresses.)

5. Income other than from operation of business.

What amount of income, other than from operation of your business, have you received during each of the 2 years immediately preceding the filing of the original petition herein?
(Give particulars, including each source, and the amount received therefrom.)

6. Tax returns and refunds.

a. In whose possession are copies of your federal and state income tax returns for the 3 years immediately preceding the filing of the original petition herein?

b. What tax refunds (income or other) have you received during the 2 years immediately preceding the filing of the original petition herein?

c. To what tax refunds (income or other), if any, are you, or may you be, entitled?
(Give particulars, including information as to any refund payable jointly to you and your spouse or any other person.)

Form No. 8. statement of affairs: engaged in business: page 1. 10-79

3078 Form No. 8, page 1

© 1979 JULIUS BLUMBERG, INC.

7. Bank accounts and safe deposit boxes.

a. What bank accounts have you maintained, alone or together with any other person, and in your own or any other name, within the 2 years immediately preceding the filing of the original petition herein?

(Give the name and address of each bank, the name in which the deposit was maintained, and the name and address of every person authorized to make withdrawals from such account.)

b. What safe deposit box or boxes or other depository or depositories have you kept or used for your securities, cash, or other valuables within the 2 years immediately preceding the filing of the original petition herein?

(Give the name and address of the bank or other depository, the name in which each box or other depository was kept, the name and address of every person who had the right of access thereto, a description of the contents thereof, and, if the box has been surrendered, state when surrendered or, if transferred, when transferred and the name and address of the transferee.)

8. Property held for another person.

What property do you hold for any other person?

(Give name and address of each person, and describe the property, the amount or value thereof and all writings relating thereto.)

9. Prior bankruptcy proceedings.

What cases under the Bankruptcy Act or title 11, United States Code have previously been brought by or against you?

(State the location of the bankruptcy court, the nature and number of the case, and whether a discharge was granted or refused, the case was dismissed, or a composition, arrangement, or plan was confirmed.)

10. Receiverships, general assignments, and other modes of liquidation.

a. Was any of your property, at the time of the filing of the original petition herein, in the hands of a receiver, trustee, or other liquidating agent?

(If so, give a brief description of the property and the name and address of the receiver, trustee, or other agent, and, if the agent was appointed in a court proceeding, the name and location of the court, the title and number of the case, and the nature thereof.)

b. Have you made any assignment of your property for the benefit of your creditors, or any general settlement with your creditors, within the 2 years immediately preceding the filing of the original petition herein?

(If so, give dates, the name and address of the assignee, and a brief statement of the terms of assignment or settlement.)

11. Property in hands of third person.

Is any other person holding anything of value in which you have an interest?

(Give name and address, location and description of the property, and circumstances of the holding.)

12. Suits, executions, and attachments.

a. Were you a party to any suit pending at the time of the filing of the original petition herein?

(If so, give the name and location of the court and the title and number of the case, and nature of the proceeding.).

b. Were you a party to any suit terminated within the year immediately preceding the filing of the original petition herein?

(If so, give the name and location of the court, the title and nature of the proceeding, and the result.)

c. Has any of your property been attached, garnished, or seized under any legal or equitable process within the year immediately preceding the filing of the original petition herein?

(If so, describe the property seized or person garnished, and at whose suit.)

13. Payments on loans and installment purchases.

What repayments on loans in whole or in part, and what payments on installment purchases of goods and services, have you made during the year immediately preceding the filing of the original petition herein?

(Give the names and addresses of the persons receiving payment, the amounts of the loans and of the purchase price of the goods and services, the dates of the original transactions, the amounts and dates of payments, and, if any of the payees are your relatives or insiders, the relationship; if the debtor is a partnership and any of the payees is or was a partner or a relative of a partner, state the relationship; if the debtor is a corporation and any of the payees is or was an officer, director, or stockholder, or a relative of an officer, director, or stockholder, state the relationship.)

14. Transfers of property.

a. Have you made any gifts, other than ordinary and usual presents to family members and charitable donations, during the year immediately preceding the filing of the original petition herein?

(If so, give names and addresses of donees and dates, description, and value of gifts.)

b. Have you made any other transfer, absolute or for the purpose of security, or any other disposition which was not in the ordinary course of business during the year immediately preceding the filing of the original petition herein?

(Give a description of the property, the date of the transfer or disposition, to whom transferred or how disposed of, and state whether the transferee is a relative, partner, shareholder, officer, director or insider, the consideration, if any, received for the property, and the disposition of such consideration.)

Form No. 8, statement of affairs: engaged in business: page 2, 10-79

3078 Form No. 8, page 2

© 1979 JULIUS BLUMBERG, INC.

15. Accounts and other receivables.
Have you assigned, either absolutely or as security, any of your accounts or other receivables during the year immediately preceding the filing of the original petition herein?
(If so, give names and addresses of assignees.)

16. Repossessions and returns.
Has any property been returned to, or repossessed by, the seller or by a secured party during the year immediately preceding the filing of the original petition herein?
(If so, give particulars, including the name and address of the party getting the property and its description and value.)

17. Business leases.
If you are a tenant of business property, what is the name and address of your landlord, the amount of your rental, the date to which rent had been paid at the time of the filing of the original petition herein, and the amount of security held by the landlord?

18. Losses.
a. Have you suffered any losses from fire, theft, or gambling during the year immediately preceding the filing of the original petition herein?
(If so, give particulars, including dates, names, and places, and the amounts of money or value and general description of property lost.)
b. Was the loss covered in whole or part by insurance?
(If so, give particulars.)

19. Withdrawals.
a. If you are an individual proprietor of your business, what personal withdrawals of any kind have you made from the business during the year immediately preceding the filing of the original petition herein?
b. If the debtor is a partnership or corporation, what withdrawals, in any form (including compensation, bonuses or loans), have been made or received by any member of the partnership, or by any officer, director, insider, managing executive, or shareholder of the corporation, during the year immediately preceding the filing of the original petition herein?
(Give the name and designation or relationship to the debtor of each person, the dates and amounts of withdrawals, and the nature or purpose thereof.)

20. Payments or transfers to attorneys.
a. Have you consulted an attorney during the year immediately preceding or since the filing of the original petition herein?
(Give date, name, and address.)
b. Have you during the year immediately preceding or since the filing of the original petition herein paid any money or transferred any property to the attorney, or to any other person on his behalf?
(If so, give particulars, including amount paid or value of property transferred and date of payment or transfer.)
c. Have you, either during the year immediately preceding or since the filing of the original petition herein, agreed to pay any money or transfer any property to an attorney at law, or to any other person on his behalf?
(If so, give particulars, including amount and terms of obligation.)

(If the debtor is a partnership or corporation, the following additional question should be answered.)

21. Members of partnership; officers, directors, managers, and principal stockholders of corporation.
a. What is the name and address of each member of the partnership, or the name, title, and address of each officer, director, insider, and managing executive, and of each stockholder holding 20 per cent or more of the issued and outstanding stock, of the corporation?
b. During the year immediately preceding the filing of the original petition herein, has any member withdrawn from the partnership, or any officer, director, insider, or managing executive of the corporation terminated his relationship, or any stockholder holding 20 per cent or more of the issued stock disposed of more than 50 per cent of his holdings?
(If so, give name and address and reason for withdrawal, termination, or disposition, if known.)
c. Has any person acquired or disposed of 20 per cent or more of the stock of the corporation during the year immediately preceding the filing of the petition?
(If so, give name and address and particulars.)

Unsworn Declaration under Penalty of Perjury

I *(We)* and

certify under penalty of perjury that I *(we)* have read the foregoing schedules, consisting of sheets, and that they are true and correct to the best of my *(our)* knowledge, information, and belief.

Executed on 19

Signature

Signature

Form No. 8 statement of affairs: engaged in business: page 3, 10-79

* Person certifying for partnership or corporation should indicate position or relationship to debtor.
3078 Form No. 8, page 3

© 1979 JULIUS BLUMBERG, INC.

Glossary

Accommodation Putting one's name on a note without any consideration or personal benefit, with the intention of lending one's own credit to that of the party accommodated.

Arrangement An agreement between debtor and creditors for extended payment and/or reduction of all or some of the debts affected by the proceeding.

Attachment Taking property into legal custody at the initiation of a lawsuit as security for payment of any judgement.

Bankruptcy Proceedings undertaken in a federal court when a debtor is unable to pay his/her debts or to reach an agreement with creditors outside of court.

Chapter (of bankruptcy law) Chapters 1, 3, and 5 cover general administration. Chapter 7 covers liquidation. Chapter 11 covers reorganization, and Chapter 13 covers adjustment of debts of individuals with regular income.

Chattel Mortgage A written instrument by which the owner transfers conditional title to personal property to secure the payment of a debt or other obligation.

Claim The right to payment or right to remedy in case of breach of performance.

Composition An agreement between debtor and creditors in which the creditors agree to accept less than the full amount of their claim. Payments may be made either in a lump sum or over a period of time.

Conditional Sales Contract An agreement to pay a debt secured by the merchandise purchased.

Confirmation The referee's (judge's) approval of the debtor's proposed payment plan.

Consideration Whatever is paid to one person in order to acquire property, money, or other services from another. It may be money or property, but could be a promise to perform or not to perform an act.

Consumer Debt Debt incurred by an individual primarily for a personal, family, or household purpose.

Contingent Possible, but dependent upon the occurrence of some future event, which is uncertain or questionable.

Conveyance A transfer of property by a written document, such as a deed in the case of real property.

Deficiency Judgement A judgement that creditors can obtain when the proceeds from the sale of collateral is insufficient to pay a secured debt.

Discharge The release of the debtor from paying the balances of his/her debts after non-exempt assets are distributed. Does not eliminate debts which are non-dischargeable under the Bankruptcy Act.

Encumbrance A claim against property.

Equity The value of a property over and above what is owed on it. Equity Security is a share in a corporation, interest in a limited partnership, or warrants to subscribe to the above.

Executory Contract An agreement to perform some action in the future.

Exempt Assets Property which a bankrupt may keep, being unavailable for satisfying creditors' claims because of federal or state laws applying to bankruptcy proceedings.

Extension A payment plan that provides for full payment of creditors' claims, but over a longer period of time.

Fair Debt Collection Practices Act An act giving debtors additional protection against harrassment by collectors.

Fraudulent Conveyance The transfer of property by a debtor, understandingly and deliberately, to defraud, hinder, or delay his/her creditors.

Garnishment Attachment of a person's wages, part of which are paid directly from employer to creditor.

Homestead Exemption Laws Those statutes which allow a family head to designate a house and land as his/her homestead, giving it protection against seizure to satisfy general debts.

Individual with Regular Income One whose income is sufficiently stable and regular to enable individual to make payments under a plan, under Chapter 13, except for stockbrokers and commodity brokers.

Insider A person who has a sufficiently close relationship with the debtor that transactions between the two are subject to close scrutiny. In the case of an individual, this would include relatives. In a partnership, a general partner would be an insider. In a corporation, an insider would be a director, officer, or person in control of the debtor.

Insolvency Usually means the inability to pay debts as they come due. Under the Bankruptcy Act, it is usually considered to mean that a debtor's property is worth less than his/her debts.

Judgement A decision by a court as to the obligations of the parties to a lawsuit.

Levy Seize property or funds to satisfy a judgement.

Lien A creditor's interest in property which can then be used for the repayment of an obligation if the debtor defaults.

Negotiable Instrument A note which can be transferred by endorsing it. To be negotiable, an instrument must be signed, be in writing, and must contain an unconditional promise to pay a certain amount of money on demand, or at some fixed future date.

Note A written promise to pay a specific amount to a specified person.

Person Includes an individual, a partnership, and a corporation.

Preferential Payment A transfer of property or money to one creditor which would give that creditor a greater percentage of his/her debt than other creditors of the same class would receive.

Priority Creditor A creditor whose claim is in the categories specified by the Bankruptcy Act to be paid first after secured claims and expenses of administering the case have been paid.

Proof of Claim Formal establishment of a claim by written document. It provides details of amounts owed by the bankrupt, and the transactions upon which the claim is based.

Reaffirmation Agreement to renew a debt, subject to court approval.

Referee The federal official appointed to preside over bankruptcy cases, similar to a judge in other legal proceedings.

Replevin Recovery of goods by legal process.

Restraining Order An injunction (prohibition) by the court preventing a party from proceeding further, with specified actions. In the case of bankruptcy, creditors would be prohibited from maintenance of lawsuits to collect debts.

Schedules The petitioner's list of debts and assets which are required to be filed with (or shortly after) the Petition.

Secured Creditor A creditor who holds an interest in collateral as security for the payment of the debt.

Transfer Any mode of disposing of property or interest in a property.

Trustee (in bankruptcy) A person elected by creditors at a meeting held before the referee, or one appointed by the referee, to collect and distribute property of the bankrupt.

Usury Interest charged on a loan which is in excess of that allowed by law.

Bibliography

Books and Pamphlets

Better Business Bureau, *Consumer's Buying Guide*, Universal Publishing and Distributing Co., 1969.

Bogen, Jules I., Editor, *Financial Handbook*, The Ronald Press, 1965.

Burger, Robert E. and Slavlicek, Jan J., *The Layman's Guide to Bankruptcy*, Van Nostrand Reinhold Co., 1971.

Carr, Joseph, *The Power of Money Management*, Financial Publishers, 1967.

Drucker, Peter F., *The Age of Discontinuity*, Harper & Row, 1969.

Faulkner, Harold Underwood, *American Economic History*, Harper & Brothers, 1954.

Foulke, Roy A., *Practical Financial Statement Analysis*, McGraw Hill, 1961.

Groupe, Leonard M., *Going Broke and How To Avoid It*, Thomas Y. Crowell Co., 1972.

Kirk, John, *How To Manage Your Money*, The Benjamin Co., 1966.

Kling, Samuel G., *The Legal Encyclopedia*, Pocket Books, Inc., 1965.

Meyers, Jerome I., *Wipe Out Your Debts & Make A Fresh Start*, Chancellor Press, Inc., 1973.

Nicholas, Ted, *How To Form Your Own Corporation Without A Lawyer For Under $50.00*, Enterprise Publishing Co., 1974, 1980.

Rutberg, Sidney, *Ten Cents On The Dollar Or The Bankruptcy Game*, Simon & Schuster, 1973.

Stanley, David T. & Girth, Marjorie, *Bankruptcy, Problem, Process, Reform*, The Brookings Institution, 1971.

Reference Books

American Jurisprudence New Topic Service, *Rules of Bankruptcy and Official Forms*, Jurisprudence Publishers, 1974.

United States Code Annotated, revised Bankruptcy Act approved November 6, 1978, West Publishing Co.

Newspaper and Other Articles

Associated Press, *March Bankruptcies Set Record*, Wilmington Evening Journal, May 13, 1975.

Boardroom Reports, *How to Survive the Financial Squeeze*, November 15, 1979.

Brooks, Judge Gene E., *The New Bankruptcy Code*, Management Magazine, as reprinted by Associated Credit Bureaus.

Cincinnati Bar Association, *Bankruptcy Code Seminar*, June 8, 1979. *Exemptions in the Present Ohio Statutes*, Sub. H.B. #674.

Focus of Interest, *Small Businesses Fear the Effects of Tighter Credit*, October 16, 1979.

Goldman, Sachs & Co., *Investment Strategy Highlights*, various bi-monthly reports, 1975.

Hoffman, Richard J. and Steven R. Resnick, *What Happens in a Credit Crunch*, Merrill Lynch Investment Strategy, November/December, 1979.

Kenny, Carl Brock, *Is the Consumer Overextended?*, Shearson Hayden Stone, October 1, 1979, Vol. V, No. 3.

Klein, M., *The New Bankruptcy Code*, Practical Lawyer, Part I—January 15, 1979, Part II—March 1, 1979.

Kudlow, Lawrence A., *Statement on Problem of Inflation*, delivered before House Budget Committee, Task Force on Inflation, House of Representatives on June 19, 1979.

Legg Mason Washington Service, *Corporate Financial Structure and Public Policy — A Question of Equity*, January, 1975.

Paine Webber 1978 Annual Report, *Do You Sincerely Want to be Poor?*

Rankin, Deborah, *How Not to Get Too Deep in Debt*, Redbook Magazine, 1979.

Santini, Galeazzo, *Letter From Italy — Money Losers Kept On Life Machine*, The Money Manager, December 1, 1975.

Small, A Thomas, *The Bankruptcy Code from the Viewpoint of the Secured Commercial Lender*, The Journal of Commercial Bank Lending, May, 1979.

Trust, Ronald Fal, *The Discharge of Debts Under the New Bankruptcy Code*, The Practical Lawyer, June 1, 1979.

Wall Street Journal, *Taking Credit: Bankruptcy Cases to Surge With Consumer Changes*, September 27, 1979.

INDEX